Start and Run a Profitable
Secondhand Store

Start and Run a Profitable Secondhand Store

Richard Cropp
Barbara Braidwood
Susan M. Boyce

Self-Counsel Press
(a division of)
International Self-Counsel Press Ltd.

Printed in Canada

First edition: December 1997

Canadian Cataloguing in Publication Data

Cropp, Richard, 1952-
Start and run a profitable secondhand store

(Self-counsel series)
ISBN 1-55180-136-1

   1. Secondhand trade. 2. Pawnbroking. 3. New business enterprises. I. Braidwood, Barbara, 1952- II. Boyce, Susan M., 1956- III. Title. IV. Series.
HF5482.C76 1997   381.19'068   C97-910805-5

Cover photography by Terry Guscott, ATN Visuals, Vancouver, B.C.

Self-Counsel Press
(a division of)
International Self-Counsel Press Ltd.

1704 N. State Street   1481 Charlotte Road
Bellingham, WA 98225   North Vancouver, BC V7J 1H1
U.S.A.   Canada

Contents

WORKSHEETS

SAMPLES

Acknowledgments

Our thanks to all those who took the time to talk to us about their secondhand stores. Special thanks to Ed DesRoches and Kate O'Brien, Plum Clothing, Vancouver, British Columbia; Mike Dorn, Augusta Book Exchange, Augusta, Georgia; Kyle Foster, Encore Computers, North Vancouver, British Columbia; Charlisa Damron-Haag, The Wrecking Bar of Atlanta Inc., Atlanta, Georgia; Sheryl Hall, The Clothes Hanger, Martinez, Georgia; Quinn Harris, Consign It Sports, Ladner, British Columbia; Pat and Eileen Kernaghan, Neville Books, Burnaby, British Columbia; Pierre St. Denis, Vancouver, British Columbia; and Ken Wharton, Black Tie Systems Group Inc., White Rock, British Columbia, who so generously shared not only their knowledge but their stories and experiences.

Introduction

Welcome to the world of the continuous Easter egg hunt where treasure lies hidden just about anywhere. At any moment you could rub the dust from an old jug and have a financial genie pop out ready to fill your pockets with cash. Some of the history you uncover is so sad it will make you cry or so ingenious that all you can do is marvel. By choosing to open a secondhand business, you are entering a business that will, at the very least, never be boring and is often filled with amazement and wonderful surprises.

Most secondhand dealers are part Indiana Jones — searching through the past for treasure — and part steely eyed robber baron appraising the next acquisition. Most are avid collectors with their own peculiar passion, and just about all of them love to shop. They almost never tire of the hunt for the novel and unusual. They spend their day finding, buying, selling, and reading about everything from coins to dolls, from weather vanes to American eagle sculptures.

The lure of the treasure hunt has always been a major draw for people in this business. The recent discovery of a "lost" painting by an old master in someone's attic (it turned out to be fake, but this wasn't discovered until a major museum paid a stupendous amount for it) or a rusty cookie tin with someone's life savings tucked away in an old trunk has fuelled the imagination of more than one business start-up.

But rest assured, there are still many more treasures waiting to be discovered now than have been uncovered by all the antique and collectible dealers who have ever lived. Treasures such as the staddle stones (old foundation stones for corn cribs) and road mileage stones that people used to pay to have hauled away a few years ago are now worth a thousand dollars apiece. At the price mill stones are going for today, you will want one around your neck. Prices haven't just doubled or tripled in a few years as it has become more popular to buy junk; this so-called junk has now gone from being worthless to being worth a fortune, and it is out there just waiting to be discovered.

To give you some idea how BIG big really is in this business, Grow Biz International, Inc., started in 1983 as a single store and now has 1150 franchise stores in the United States and Canada. It is a publicly traded company with US$414 million in total sales and has expanded to include five different franchises, all basically secondhand (Play It Again Sports, Once Upon A Child, Computer Renaissance, Disk Around, and Music Around).

No one could have foreseen the change in public attitude that has happened in the last couple of decades. This is a renewed and vibrant industry where you can still make it big. All you have to do to cash in is read on.

Part I
The secondhand scene

1
Treasure hunting as a business

a. The resurgence of the secondhand scene

During the last 20 years, the secondhand business has changed from a mom and pop industry with a plethora of weird characters selling from the depths of dingy stores to an industry with several multi-million dollar players. Nowadays there are new personalities on the secondhand scene. Teenagers with barely a whisker are busy making money buying and selling computer components that didn't exist a decade ago but are now obsolete. Chain stores, franchises, securities dealers, and lawyers have invaded this realm of the small business person.

People still want the good life with fashionable clothes, up-to-date music for their stereos, fast computers, good quality sporting goods, all the basics and extras for the kitchen, and a living room that shows off their personal taste and style. The trouble is, most North Americans, squeezed by declining real incomes and a higher cost of living, cannot afford even what their parents could.

But buying secondhand was not really an option for extending disposable income until the 1980s, when the stigma of owning cast-offs began to weaken. People began to actually boast about finding deals such as an Alfred Sung blazer for only $10 in a secondhand consignment store.

The way people view secondhand dealers has changed dramatically, too. At one time, the stereotypical image was of beer-bellied, nicotine-stained pawnshop owners preying on the unfortunate and the down-and-out. A smell of old tennis shoes and dirty clothes always seemed to cling to them and their goods.

But as the industry reinvents itself, new public attitudes and perceptions mean secondhand store owners are finally enjoying the same respect other retailers have enjoyed for years. There are now many stores that are as tasteful as any upscale department store, with sports jacket– and tie-attired salesmen and fashionably dressed saleswomen. It is only a matter of time before there is a certain amount of glamor attached to globe trotting buyers for secondhand businesses jetting around the world looking for treasures.

A great advantage to starting a secondhand business is that few businesses can be started with absolutely no cash and built into multi-million dollar companies: a secondhand business can. You already have the products for your first day of selling in your closet. Many successful secondhand business people started simply with a garage sale from time to time and progressed to a store front and then to several locations. Start-up expenses can be kept extremely low — no rent, phone, employees, electricity bills, or government papers to fill out — and the profit margins are so good that it doesn't take much to generate all the cash you may need to sustain the business as it goes along.

Starting tiny is a great way to learn the business without risking a large sum of money and a large amount of valuable time. Without the pressure of supporting an expensive storefront, learning the trade can be done at your own pace. By working on your business on a part-time basis, you can find out if you really like the buying and selling or if it is best left as a hobby. It is also easier to pick your own timing for a move to a bigger business. If life's demands make it inconvenient to take on the commitment of opening a store, you can simply wait and continue to earn extra cash, hone your skills, and do your research with your part-time business.

b. The "green" component

At first it was a trend most people viewed as "one of those hippie things" we could laughingly tolerate and mostly ignore. Today, more and more people are realizing that recycling is an important step in preserving our planet.

Industry analysts say the trend toward recycling and reusing, and the urgent need most middle-class consumers feel to stretch their dollars has given secondhand businesses the biggest boost since the Romans recycled all those Greek temples a few thousand years ago. More likely this has been a revolt of practical parents in our society who finally refuse to pay increasingly outrageous prices for a pair of sports shoes which would see their soccer-playing child through one season — if they were lucky. By buying gently used goods, parents can give themselves and their children the very best quality for a few months and then turn the goods in for a partial refund at the local secondhand store.

This ecological concern is cited by a surprising number of secondhand dealers as one of the reasons they got into the business. "We have to look at the global sustainability of a society based on consumerism," points out one successful sporting goods owner. "Especially in Western society, we're encouraged not only to throw stuff out as soon as we're done with it, but to buy far more than we could possibly need in the first place and throw the excess away unused. Consignment and secondhand stores help people get into a different mind-set, one that says it's good to repair and reuse. Even though I know that may not be the prime consideration when my customers first walk in the door, I'm still helping to educate them in a different direction. And I can earn a decent living doing it, too."

c. *Professional treasure hunters please enquire within*

If you spend any time around secondhand dealers, you'll soon come to an important realization. No matter what they are selling, people who go into the secondhand business love the thrill of treasure hunting. In fact, sometimes the thrill of the hunt is the most important part of the whole business. And because running a secondhand store is all about treasure hunting every day, secondhand dealers are absolutely passionate about what they do.

This passion usually grows out of personal interest, whether it is in books, computers, or small figurines of one-eyed pirates with purple tunics. Over and over, successful dealers relate tales of collecting specific items since the time they remember being old enough to have pocket money. Many also confess to an overwhelming inability to throw things out. The next logical step is inevitably opening a store to specialize in the same collectibles.

Secondhand stores are the ultimate way to reuse and recycle.

People the world over are awakening to the fact that some of their garbage is worth something to those "crazy North Americans." The Japanese have legions of searchers prowling secondhand and goodwill stores in North America looking for used sneakers which bring thousands of dollars a pair in Japan.

If this description fits you, you'll likely already have one important asset: a head start on gaining the vast knowledge about your subject that you'll need to be successful. "Some people think they can just hang out a sign and they're in business," says one paperback book trader. "If you're going to go into the used book business, sure you have to love books, but you have to know the difference between Ludlum and Dickens, too, if you're going to be successful."

However, having an encyclopedia in your head does not mean months or years of specialized training. In fact, most dealers are primarily self-taught. They read voraciously, they frequent other stores, they research, and they talk to people. "You can learn a lot from your customers," report secondhand dealers of all types. And the good news is that most people are more than willing to share their knowledge with you for nothing more than the joy of sharing.

One of the most intriguing aspects of the world of secondhand turns out to be almost indefinable. It's the zest for living that's typical of everyone in the business — an enjoyment of life's quirky twists and turns that are celebrated and shared.

Like the general goods dealer who talks about the day he found an Alex Colville landscape sandwiched between a velvet painting of a Mexican woman holding a smoking rifle and a framed poster listing several dozen of Murphy's more twisted laws.

"I wasn't sure at first it was actually a Colville," he says. "But I knew it was a good painting and one that would sell even if it wasn't authentic. When I found out it was the real thing, I couldn't resist. I hung it on my living room wall for six months just so I could say I'd actually owned an original Alex Colville."

It didn't matter that he eventually sold the painting at a very tidy profit. What really made this man's eyes twinkle was just being able to celebrate the fact that he *had* owned an Alex Colville.

Another intriguing aspect of the business is the "best sale" story from a dealer who was contacted by a woman who wanted all her son's belongings out of the house. What prompted the abrupt purging wasn't clear, but she was insistent: everything had to go. When the dealer arrived, he discovered an antique opthamologist's chair sitting majestically in the middle of the living room floor. "I thought it was funky," he confesses with a good-natured shrug, "so I bought it for $25 and then had to spend an hour and a half taking the thing to pieces so I could get it in my car."

The world is so full of a number of things, I'm sure we should all be as happy as kings.

Robert Louis Stevenson

Back in his store, the chair was set up (after another couple of hours piecing it back together) in a place of honor in the front window. For two weeks people passed by barely noticing it. "Then one day a youngish guy in a BMW came into the store practically leaping up and down with excitement. "I just have to have this," he said, fondling the leather seat. He asked how much I wanted for it. I told him I'd never seen one before, but I figured it had to be worth $2,000." The man blanched, muttered something about it being more than he wanted to pay, and walked out of the store.

But, so the story goes, he didn't drive away. He sat in the car, he got out again and paced up and down in front of the store. He got back in his car — the antics went on for ten minutes. "Finally," says the dealer, "he pulled his wallet out, thumbed through it, and came back in. He offered me $1,200 cash on the spot if I'd help him load it into the back of his BMW. I'm still not sure how we managed to cram it in the trunk, but he drove away a happy man, and you'd better believe I celebrated too."

Sure some doubters will say it's eccentricity, others will roll their eyes and make odd clucking sounds, but the truth is that, on the whole, secondhand dealers are an irrepressibly happy group. Whether their chosen profession is the thing that makes them happy is anyone's guess, but it is an almost universal trait among dealers of all sorts. And in the end, it may be one of the greatest bonuses of any career choice.

Here are some tips to expand your knowledge base as you determine — and then possibly expand — your product line.

d. Secondhand opportunities

There are almost unlimited opportunities to specialize in secondhand goods. Several of the most common are discussed in detail in the upcoming chapters, but there are successful secondhand stores devoted to almost every type of product imaginable. Here are just a few:

- *Dolls.* From rag dolls to Barbie dolls to exquisite porcelain and lace dolls, these toys have enjoyed ongoing popularity among children and adults alike. Although the first thought is that dolls are mainly for little girls, there is a whole range of "dolls for boys" as well. Collectors have been known to pay top dollar for GI Joe dolls in good condition.

- *Toys.* A world of endless fascination for kids of all ages.

- *Sports cards*. Active trading isn't just among players moving from team to team. Sports cards are hot items and don't take up a lot of space to store.

- *CDs, tapes, and records*. There's a booming market in old recordings of all types.

- *Stereo equipment*. Like computers, this is especially good if you like to tinker with electronic equipment.

- *China*. Ask culinary experts and most will say that atmosphere is part of any good meal. And that means a complete set of matching china for many people. Unfortunately for them, but very fortunately for you, patterns are discontinued on a regular basis, making it all but impossible to replace a broken dinner plate or teacup without the services of a dealer in fine china.

- *Silverware*. Silverware is often, but far from always, combined with fine china.

- *Pens and writing instruments*. Not just for authors — many people want more than a 49¢ ballpoint.

- *Brand name products*. Coca Cola, Disney products, and even Ronald McDonald and his famous gang are just three examples of brand names that have spawned new opportunities for specialized stores.

- *Movies, television, and the theater*. From Sinatra to *Sesame Street* to *Sunset Boulevard*, people are intrigued by the world of entertainment. Posters and all sorts of other memorabilia are much sought after by many collectors.

- *Military history*. You don't have to carry three suits of armor and a couple of cannons to appeal to historically minded people. Uniforms, medals, old photos, and even buttons can all give you a basic stock to begin your store.

- *Limited edition collector plates*. An almost unbelievable range of subject and style exists in the world of collector plates. But don't forget that without the original box and certificate of authenticity, these may suddenly become almost worthless.

e. *Reference books*

Keep a sharp eye out for current reference books and read them faithfully. Every industry has standard reference books showing sale prices, asking prices, hallmarks, and other ways to identify quality product, histories, and a host of other useful information.

Many of these books are updated annually (in some cases, even more frequently) and will give you an authoritative reference when it comes to pricing your own product. Check with other people who specialize in the same area as you want to, and find out which reference books they find most useful. Appendix 1 will also give you a jump start on reference guides for a variety of subjects.

f. Industry magazines

Invest in a couple of subscriptions to magazines geared to your specialty and read them faithfully. Trade publications, even if they are targeted primarily to retailers who sell new product, are one of the easiest and most reliable ways to keep you up-to-date on pricing and hot new buying trends. There will always be a market for items that have fallen from favor in the public's eye, and more and more people are looking to secondhand stores to help them keep up-to-date for less money than buying new. If you don't know what the current trends are, you will be missing a huge section of the market.

A selection of industry-specific reference books and a couple of subscriptions to specialty trade magazines are essential tools if you want to compete in the collectibles marketplace.

g. The cyclical nature of goods

Some goods enjoy a cyclical popularity. Sometimes this means an article that has fallen out of favor in the public eye will suddenly move right back in line with modern trends and become very salable. For example, the chrome and plastic look popular in the late 1950s and early 1960s enjoyed a brief but strong surge of interest in the early 1990s. Keeping up-to-date on what's happening in the industry will allow you to spot these trends.

h. Get involved with industry associations

It may take some digging, but you will usually be able to find an association devoted to your particular interest. If it holds regular meetings, try to go as a guest for a couple of times before you join so that you have the opportunity to check out the association.

Associations may also sponsor industry trade fairs, which are another excellent source of both knowledge and networking opportunities, especially if you have a very tight focus in what you sell.

Try to get on a few mailing lists and attend at least a couple of shows each year. As your sales begin to generate steady income, you might also want to consider a booth of your own.

i. Encourage people to share their knowledge with you

Your customers are often an excellent source of insider information.

Everyone has a vast store of knowledge about certain subjects. But it tends to be part of human nature that we downplay the value of our own experience and expertise. When this gets combined with preconceived ideas about who would be knowledgeable on certain subjects, it can often mean lost opportunities for learning.

For example, one used stereo and music store owner from Toronto had a customer (18 years old) who regularly came with eight-track tape decks and cassettes for sale. At first the owner was suspicious because "the kid looked like a thug." After a while, he realized the young man simply had a very good eye for quality stereo equipment and liked to do the garage sale route.

But the real surprise didn't happen for about a year. One day when the teenager came in with a couple of tape decks, the dealer was on the phone. The call took ten minutes, and when it was finally over, he discovered his young supplier browsing through the classical section. "It turned out that the kid knew more about the classics than anyone I'd ever had working in the store," the owner says with a chuckle. "My part-time sales gal had just quit, so I couldn't pass up an opportunity like that. I hired him on the spot. He worked for me for a couple of years, and I learned more interesting stuff about Brahms and his buddies in those two years than I had from any book."

While not everyone will turn out to be a store assistant and library all in one, don't overlook simple conversation as an excellent source of important information.

2
Books

Behind the counter of most secondhand bookstores you'll find a person who's passionate about books — the way books feel, the stories they tell, the illustrations, the scent of old leather and parchment, the way books fit in the hand. Many bookstores originated from personal collections which outgrew the available space at home. In fact, most secondhand book dealers if they aren't helping a customer or out hunting for new treasures can usually be found with their nose buried in a book off their shelves.

Books are also one of the few commodities people seem to have no built-in bias against purchasing secondhand. After all, for centuries people have been reading books which have been read by countless other people, thereby producing that incredible institution called a lending library. It's only one step in a slightly different direction to open a secondhand bookstore.

"In books for to rede I me delite"

Inscription on an art deco bookcase

a. Finding product

The main source of books for a bookseller is individuals selling their books. Other sources include church rummage sales, flea markets, and estate sales. Of these, estate sales are probably the most common and useful, as the other two are often flooded with Harlequin romances, Reader's Digests, and old product that isn't in demand. Auctions are not usually a great source of supply, with the exception of first editions or other rare books.

If your store will accept trade-ins, a sign advertising this either outside or in a prominent position inside is useful. If you plan to do any formal advertising, mention in the ad that you accept trade-ins.

b. How much do I buy it for?

Establishing a purchase price for paperback books you buy from clients — often individuals trying to sell their books — is usually much simpler than for hardcovers, which generally must be priced individually. Relatively current paperback books most commonly sell for approximately half the cover price. This means you can calculate your purchase price based on the markup you decide you need. See chapter 18 for more details on markup and pricing tips.

Another popular form of payment is store credit. Often, booksellers offer sellers a choice between cash payment outright or credit against in-store purchases. There are advantages and disadvantages to allowing store credit. Chapter 17 discusses it in more detail.

c. What do I accept?

Many dealers do not stock Harlequin romances or Reader's Digest Condensed Books because it's easy to become overrun by them. These mass-produced publications are also readily available in hospital auxiliary stores and garage sales at prices few bookstores can afford to match.

Many used bookstores start with an interest in a specific subject; military history, science fiction, children's literature, and mystery are common subjects. This makes the choice of what to buy simple. But as your store becomes better known, people will want to sell you books of all kinds. Variety will make your store appealing to more readers, but as you branch out, watch closely for subjects that sit on the shelves for months on end. Initially you will have to rely on instinct — that gut feeling that a certain type of book will sell in your area. Sometimes your instinct will be wrong. But these initial mistakes will also help you become more selective and accurate.

d. Beware: hungry cat on premises

At first glance, it's tempting to think fire would be the biggest hazard to a secondhand bookstore. In reality, fire is no more a consideration for a bookstore than for any other store. After all, wooden dressers and buffets burn just as well as paper.

The two most deadly perils to a bookstore owner according to most dealers? Mice and water.

Mice love to feast on the spines of leather-bound books or nibble on delicate page corners at midnight. And while mousetraps and poison usually solve the problem, a surprising number of book dealers have discovered a cuddly tabby or lazy, brown-eyed basset hound makes a great companion, promotes conversation with customers, and is often more effective than mechanical methods of controlling these rodents.

The true bane of all booksellers is water. A leak from the floor above can drip over dozens of shelves, turning their treasures into soggy mush. Water is also fickle. Sometimes it will run the entire length of a shelf, merrily bypassing dozens of Michael Crichton novels only to soak through thousands of pages of Stephen King.

Here are some tips to help minimize your risk of water damage:

(a) As you check over a potential location, be sure to feel the walls, especially the outer walls. If they are damp, your product will soon suffer the same fate. Condensation on window panes is another tip off to an environment bad for books.

(b) What is above the store? An apartment with a leaky bathtub or a toilet that's prone to back up is trouble waiting to happen. Be sure you check for water stains on the ceiling.

(c) If you have to go down several steps to get into the store, find out where the water table is. Some areas located near the ocean or a river have a water table level no more than several inches below the surface. While this is a gardener's dream come true, it can easily become a bookseller's nightmare during the rainy season.

(d) Never store your books directly on the floor. Shelving should be raised at least an inch or two. The small-sized concrete blocks used for patios are a cheap and effective way of doing this; or cut several lengths of 2 x 4s and place your shelves on top of these.

e. Dewey decimal move over

Organizing books is one of your simpler tasks. Most stores sort first by subject and then by author. This allows you to see at a glance if you already have 25 copies of the title someone is trying to sell you 6 more of. It also lets your customers find things easily.

A notable exception are stores that carry dated manuals. These books are usually arranged by manufacturer, model, and date. For example, a store specializing in auto repair manuals might sort its books first by manufacturer (Ford, GMC, Toyota, etc.), then by model (Celica, Corolla, Tercel, etc.), and finally by year.

Of course, there are people who use the "anywhere it fits" method. This entails putting books anywhere there's currently room: on the floor, on the table, on the desk, on the cat . . . You get the picture. Surprisingly, there are a number of well-established secondhand stores that have used this method successfully for years. However, if you are serious about running a profitable store, it is not recommended.

f. Cleaning

Books often come complete with dust, dirt, and gummy spots from old price tags. The good news is that in most cases you won't need anything more than a soft rag just barely damp with soapy water to tidy up your product. For those persistent glue spots, put a small amount of lighter fluid on a cloth or piece of paper towel and rub gently until the glue lifts off.

Some dealers like to protect their more valuable books with plastic slip covers. Although it protects rare works from dust and fingerprints, the covers can sometimes be awkward to take on and off and, in some cases, cause extra wear and tear. But if you have a one-of-a-kind book, protective covers may be a necessity to protect your investment.

g. Color coding

Color coding of books is usually done for one of two reasons. Some dealers color code to keep track of how long a book has been in the store. They might use orange dots for the first quarter of a year, green for April through June, yellow for July through September, and so on. This provides an easy visual check for those shelf hogs that you should be setting out in the $.50 bin.

Other dealers prefer to use color coding to indicate price. Yellow might indicate a $4.00 book, red a $3.00 book, and purple a $1.50 book. This works fine if you only carry paperbacks, because there is a relatively small range of prices. Color coding for price is less effective for hardcovers where prices can vary dramatically according to size, age, condition, edition, and even subject matter. Post signs in strategic places throughout the store and at the cash register to tell customers which color means what price.

h. Do you have a copy?

"I'm looking for a book written by an English officer returning from the Napoleonic wars. I'm not sure what the name of the book is or who the officer was, but I know he stopped in a tiny hamlet somewhere in France, or maybe it was Spain. Anyway, he liked the place so much he ended up staying there and opening a pub. Eventually he wrote down the stories all the other returning soldiers told and then published them as a book. Have you got a copy or do you know where I could find one?"

An unlikely scenario? Not at all. If you're planning to open a used bookstore, get ready to field questions like this every day. "People tend to think we're rather like a library and use us as a reference," says one nine-year veteran secondhand bookseller who actually had a buyer phone with this question. But the bookseller was also quick to offer the reassurance that after a short while, you'll find you *do* remember titles, authors, and even what the covers look like.

Be ready for lots of enquiries from people who think you're a combination of librarian, encyclopedia, and research center.

i. Coffee, donuts, and a damn good read

A growing trend in bookstores, new and used, is a combination coffee shop/lounge and a bookstore. The jury is still out on this one. Some dealers swear it increases sales dramatically, others find all it increases is the number of lookie-loos who like free coffee and keep their money in their pockets.

If you decide to explore this option, you'll want several places people can sit, and some good reading lights. A small kitchen table and a few chairs work just as well as a comfy sofa, with the added bonus that browsers have a place to put their cup. It's also less tempting for them to curl up for the entire afternoon using your stock as library material.

If the thought of charging outright for this extra service makes you squirm, you may want to consider a "donations" bowl beside the cream and sugar. Most people will happily chip in enough to cover the cost of their java fix.

j. Advertising

For most booksellers in the secondhand business, the local Yellow Pages is their most cost-effective form of advertising. In fact, many do not bother with any other type of written advertising at all.

One store approaching its half-century celebration maximizes this avenue by listing under half a dozen different names, mostly beginning with the letters A, B, or C. For example, there might be one listing under "Al's Bookstore," one under "Bob's Bookstore," and a third under "Charlie's Bookstore." That way, all the names are found early in the Yellow Pages and a buyer is sure to see them. "We're not only one of the first names people come across," explains the manager, "but they're bound to find one of our listings eventually, no matter where they start looking in the listings."

The second most popular form of advertising is in small, local newspapers, especially in the freebie "cultural" papers that pop up in every city, town, and village. "Book buyers seem to be drawn to this type of publication," says one bookseller. "It's hard to pinpoint exactly why, but it definitely is so."

Flyers and discount coupons usually receive lukewarm reviews from recipients and appear to be heavily tied in with the demographics of a specific area. If you find you have a steady supply of discount or two-for-one offers from merchants around you, try a small test run of your own. Even if it just increases awareness of your store, it may be a worthwhile investment.

For specialty store owners, trade shows can provide an unexpected source of both exposure and sales. One store that focuses on books about collectibles and antiques regularly takes a booth at the local tri-annual antique show. Novice collectors often snap up its books on everything from dolls to daggers through the ages to use as references when negotiating with the owner of the booth around the corner.

k. What do you mean it's worthless? It's a hundred years old!

A common misconception is that "old" means "valuable." And certainly in some cases, it does. In most, it doesn't. "So many people bring in a book that's been printed in, say, the late 1800s, because they think it will be worth a lot," says one dealer. "What they don't realize is that old doesn't necessarily mean rare or in good condition."

Here are a few pointers for anyone considering the world of rare books:

(a) Most, but by no means all, publishers indicate the edition number on the same page as the copyright information and ISBN.

(b) Both the first edition and the first trade edition are sometimes simply marked as "First edition." These are not necessarily considered to be of equal value.

(c) Sometimes book rights will be purchased by a second printing house. So even though the book has enjoyed several editions already, it may be labeled a first edition when the second publisher produces its first print run.

(d) Some authors are published first in paperback and then in hardcover. One school of thought is that the paperback run doesn't count, a second school of thought is that you must differentiate between first edition in paperback or first edition in hardcover, and yet a third is that the first print run is the only true first edition, whether the book was put out in paperback or not.

(e) If the author and/or publishing house has lots of financial backing behind a book, they may produce a limited first edition that rarely, if ever, gets into the hands of the general public. These are traditionally very fancy — often sporting gold leaf on the page edges and luxurious leather bindings.

(f) Book clubs sometimes bring out their own first editions. These are usually a slightly different size than the original and are worthless to a collector. A small mark on the back cover of a book will alert you to book club offerings. Be warned, though; these marks are usually very small, often only a tiny star or a recessed dot, and are extremely difficult to spot.

Becoming an expert on rare books and first editions is like any other study — it takes years to accomplish. "It's an extremely complex subject. You can't think of it as an exact science," says one collector. "Many older books have no markings at all to show they are a first edition. Making friends with someone who already knows a lot about the subject will teach you the basics, but you're definitely going to need reference books."

3

Glad rags: the booming trend in pre-worn clothing

Every office has one. The impeccable dresser. No matter what the season or the weather, her clothes (yes, most of them are women) are designer quality, and she seems to have an endless supply of color coordinated new outfits. Coworkers speculate about how she can afford them on her salary. Perhaps she has a rich boyfriend or a millionaire in the family. Chances are, her real secret is that she simply knows where to shop for quality used clothing.

The stigma attached to buying secondhand clothing is disappearing. "At one time people would never admit to buying something secondhand," says one manager. "Now they're proud to say they got a $200 blazer for only $45 at a consignment store. All of a sudden people are really smartening up in their shopping habits and refusing to pay the price of buying new."

Used clothing is primarily targeted to a female market. While stores selling used clothing for men aren't completely unheard of, they are definitely a rarity in the marketplace. Speculation about why this is so includes:

- Men's fashions don't change as dramatically or as frequently from year to year as women's fashions do.

- Men tend to wear their clothes, especially good clothes, far longer than women wear theirs.

- Men don't like shopping for clothing, and they aren't willing to spend the time it takes going through several secondhand stores to find a suit they like. They want to go to one store, buy three items, and go home with their purchases ready to hang in the closet and wear the next day.

- It's part of a self-perpetuating cycle: men don't think about buying secondhand because there aren't many stores available, so secondhand men's clothing stores can't survive, which means there aren't stores where men can shop . . . .

This may sound sexist and politically incorrect, but it's a fact of life. If you want to open a secondhand clothing store, you will be handling mainly women's clothing.

a. *Fashions love encore performances*

It's long been known that fashions fall in and out of favor in a five to ten year cycle. The old joke about keeping it in your closet for a decade and you'll be back on the cutting edge of high fashion has a strong basis in reality, as one dealer discovered. One dealer recalls a young woman coming into her store with an arm load of clothes. "Most of them I couldn't take because they were too worn or they just weren't in fashion any more," she says. "But one of the last items was a white tuxedo dress trimmed with gold braid that still had the original price tag on it. Tuxedo dresses had just come into fashion and were selling new for $100 and up. But the tag on this woman's dress said $12.95! My guess is it was at least 20 years old but had never been worn. I got rid of the tag, and it sold in less than three days for $48."

This, of course, was an unusual case. Under normal circumstances, you'll want to avoid fashions more than two years old, and some owners have a policy that it can't be older than last year's designs. A few exceptions to the two-year rule include:

- Exceptionally high quality, designer labels

- Classics, such as the plain A-line skirt, which never really go out of style

- Evening wear

As you learn more about your clientele's preferences, you'll be able to gauge how much flexibility you will need to have with the age of garments you accept.

b. Finding product

While you can sometimes pick up good quality clothing at garage sales and flea markets, almost all stores rely exclusively on people bringing garments in. It seems to be accepted that the time and effort isn't worthwhile looking for other sources.

c. Eye/label coordination

True, it's a bit of a Hollywood cliché — the leggy, ash blonde with dark sunglasses and 50-carat diamond earrings. "Why daaarling," you can almost hear her drawling. "I wouldn't be caught dead wearing anything that wasn't _____!" (Insert your choice of fashion designers.) Most people can chuckle over the image, but there is still a mystique to fashion labels. And if the jacket still says "Alfred Sung," you'll get a higher price whether it's secondhand or not.

"It's amazing how many people bring in clothing with the labels cut off," says one dealer holding up a burgundy dress. "I know this is a Rouie because the consignor brought in an identical one in blue. Sure I'd be able to tell it's good quality just by looking at it and feeling the material, but if she'd left the label on, I'd be able to sell it for double what I'll have to mark it down to without the label. We'd both make more money off it if she'd keep her scissors in the sewing chest."

Another problem for both you and your customers is that the labels also show size and washing instructions. Not knowing the size can cost time and frustration when a customer is trying on clothing, but ultimately it is only an annoyance. Not knowing the proper care of a garment, however, can ruin it and sometimes everything else in the laundry. The fake silk that wasn't fake at all, the wash-and-wear blouse that required dry cleaning, or the colorfast blue pants that ran all over the white jogging pants — knowing the proper washing instructions avoids these disasters.

If you aren't well versed on the big-name labels, spend some time browsing through high-fashion stores in your area. You'll likely have to fend off a few sales clerks, but you'll end up with a good working knowledge of who's in and who's out in fashion labels. There are also a number of televised fashion programs worth checking out, as well as hundreds of publications covering fashions trends of all sorts, available at any library.

"You'll also find that just by working with labels you start to know the big names," adds one assistant. "When I started here about eight months ago, I hardly knew any of the big designers. Now I'm doing 90% of all the pricing for the store."

d. *Running with your intuition*

Even if the labels have been cut out, the quality of the garment will show in its construction and fabric. Here are some things to watch for when you are looking at potential product.

- Are there any frayed spots? Frays are often an indication of excessive wear or poor manufacture. Both should be avoided.

- Are all the seams and hemlines intact? Everyone's done it at some time in their life. One quick tug on a dangling thread and the entire garment falls to pieces. You don't want this happening to your stock.

- Are hemlines straight? Uneven hems can be the result of poor manufacturing or a fabric that droops as it ages. Either way, while there have been a few fashions that included wavy hemlines, as a rule, people want their skirts and pant legs to be the same length all round. You'll soon develop an eye for this, but if you're at all unsure, just grab your tape measure and run a quick check.

- Are there perspiration stains on the arm pits? If there are heavy perspiration stains or weak spots in the join between the sleeve and the body of the garment, most customers will not buy it.

- Does the neckline have stains? Necklines are famous for stains from perspiration and make-up. Both of these are hard to remove and difficult to hide when wearing the item.

- Have any repairs been made on the garment? This shouldn't automatically mean a refusal, but the repair must be small enough that it's not noticeable, and in an inconspicuous place. A blue patch half way down the front of a pink blouse is somewhat difficult to ignore when a person is wearing it. (Don't

Underclothing
(panties, bras, and
slips) generally do
not sell well in a
secondhand store.
However, lingerie
and sleepwear are
usually at least
modest sellers.

laugh; one dealer had a young woman attempt to consign just such a repaired item.)

- Are the button holes unraveling? Buttons and button holes take a lot of punishment and must be well made to stand up to the constant tugging. If the manufacturing is sloppy here, it may have been sloppy in other areas too.

e. Seasons changing — more complications

Fashion, and especially women's fashion, is closely tied to the seasons. In addition to the latest trends in style for a particular year, fabrics, length of sleeve, even color will be quite different in the fall and winter from what was popular at Easter. Here are some tips to keep your stock seasonally in tune.

- Fabric weight is one of the surest ways to place your product in the right season. The lighter fabrics will, naturally, be popular in the hotter seasons. You should begin hanging garments made of lightweight fabrics just before the weather begins to warm up so you're ready for the rush of people getting out of the winter doldrums.
- Silk is becoming a big seller year-round. In the hot weather people wear silk on its own, and in the cooler season, silk can be combined with all sorts of other fabrics.
- Floral prints generally work best in spring and summer.
- Hemlines go up in summer and down in winter for both pants and skirts.
- Sleeves are long in winter and short or nonexistent in summer.
- Bright colors tend to sell better in spring and summer than they do in fall and winter. "People are getting away from the idea that color is seasonal," says one dealer, "but it's still tough to get most people to believe it's okay to wear pink in the middle of winter."

Real silk is warm
when temperatures
drop and cool
when it rises.
This flexibility
is what made
silk so highly prized
for kimonos and
pilot's scarves.

f. Growing like weeds

Keeping kids in clothing that fits is an expensive nightmare for most parents. The child who was three foot four only yesterday seems to work through a new size of clothing every week until suddenly he or she is six foot something and still growing.

"Fast growing kids are really tough on parents," says one 13-year veteran owner of a kids consignment store, "but it means we get a steady supply of product that's barely been used. Sometimes we even have people bringing in "never been worn" items that are already too small. Lots of times an out-of-town friend will send something special like a party dress as a gift, and it isn't worth the parents' time trying to return it half way across the country. So they bring it to us."

If space is available, many secondhand kids goods stores also sell items such as cribs, toys, and books. Parents and gift-givers appreciate being able to come into your store and pick out an outfit plus a piece of furniture or something just for fun.

g. Cruising and vacation wear

One exception to the seasonal aspect of clothing is cruise and vacation wear. Cruising, especially to tropical destinations, is becoming more and more popular with all age groups. But try to find a bathing suit and a pair of shorts in Toronto or Chicago during the middle of December.

"I had so many people coming in and complaining that they couldn't find clothes for their winter cruises to the Bahamas that I decided to devote one small rack to cruise wear," says one dealer. "Within a couple of months I had to expand the section, and now I keep one wall just for vacation goers — everything from evening gowns to bathing suits and cover ups."

If your clientele likes to travel, cruise and vacation fashions can be an excellent source of revenue year-round. Be sure to mark your cruising section clearly and advertise the fact that you carry this merchandise even if it's only a big sign in the store window.

h. Controlling inventory

1. Discounting

Like most consignment stores, progressive discounting (Dutch auction) is the most popular method of ensuring your stock rotates quickly. It's best to go no more than two weeks without discounting an item between 10% and 20%. If it still hasn't sold, discount it again.

Many secondhand clothing stores use a one price, bottom-end rack to clear out leftover items. These can go as low as $1 per item,

If your location has a high percentage of retired people or upper-income executives, it may be worth your while to maintain a year-round cruise and vacation wear section.
These garments are generally night-on-the-town or hot weather styles.

but usually run between $5 and $10 each. Try putting these deep discounted racks in front of your store on the sidewalk. They are a great attention grabber to get people inside where your money-making stock is.

2. I've had this dress in my store long enough!

If it hasn't sold in 60 to 90 days, it probably won't.

You've been watching a dress you were sure would sell in no time hang on the "Just In" rack, move to the 10% Off rack, then to the 50% Off rack. Now you have it with the $5 Specials, and still no one's bought it.

After 60 to 90 days, you should be thinking about getting a garment out of your store to make room for something that will sell. You will need to indicate in your consignment contract exactly how long you are willing to keep an item before you expect the owner to pick it up. You must also consider whether or not you are willing to take the time to advise your suppliers that their goods should be picked up. By far the most common practice is to make it the consignor's responsibility to follow up on the sales progress of their property.

An interesting side note is that secondhand dealers find people rarely do come back to pick up their property after the contract time is over. "Most of them simply can't be bothered," says one dealer. "I think they consider whatever they've made by consigning it is a bonus, so they haven't really lost any money if it doesn't sell."

For most clothing, life after the $5 rack means being donated to charity. There are dozens of organizations that welcome donations of used clothing. If you aren't familiar with any in your area, contact one of your local churches. Any church is almost certain to have some suggestions.

i. Details, details

Like all businesses, it's usually the details which take the most time in running a secondhand clothing store. Here are some insider tips to help you keep everything manageable.

If you offer cleaning services, make sure you include not only the cost of the cleaning itself, but a sufficient markup to cover the cost of your time taking garments to and from the dry cleaner, or deduct the cost of cleaning from the consignor's payout.

- Insist all clothing is clean when it's brought into the store. Soiled garments won't sell. If you have any doubts, it's safer to refuse the item altogether.

  A very few dealers offer a service where they have items cleaned for their suppliers. From your point of view, this only makes sense if you are next door to a cleaner who is willing to give you an exceptionally good volume discount. In most cases, though, this is not a recommended practice.

- Clothing that's wrinkled, even when it's clean, gets passed over by customers. You'll likely want to have the ability to give your stock a quick touch up now and then, but overall, garments should be crisp and pressed when the consignee brings them in.

- It takes a deceptive amount of time to hang clothes. Most clothing stores require garments to be on hangers when they come in the store. This policy will also help eliminate pressed items becoming creased from lying in a pile in the back room waiting for pricing.

- While some stores will accept any number of items at a time, there is an increasing trend toward requiring a minimum number to be consigned at one time. This will dramatically reduce the amount of time you spend both writing new contracts and searching through the files for existing ones as items sell.

- When you hang garments, group them by type and color. For example, you might set up a rack of dresses grouped by blues, greens, and yellows. This makes it easier for the customers to find things (so you aren't always getting asked where a certain type of garment is) and makes it faster to locate a specific item if a consignor wants to remove it or a customer has come back to take a second look.

j. Jewelry and accessories

Jewelry and accessories are an easy way to increase your sales. They take up very little room, they require little special care, and people often like to pick up an accessory or a new (to them) piece of jewelry to compliment the outfit they just added to their wardrobe. "I had so many people asking for jewelry that I just couldn't afford *not* to carry it," says one dealer. And by simply converting her front counter to a display case, she didn't even have to find extra room in her already crowded store.

If you enjoy the world of fashion and have a good eye for what's quality and what isn't, a secondhand clothing store may be just your size. Besides, it's a great way to clear out your own closets!

Many stores require a minimum of six or more items to be brought in at a time.

Belts, bracelets, earrings, necklaces, scarves, and handbags are consistently fast sellers and take up very little extra space.

4
Computers

The computer industry is booming. Long vanished are the days when computers were only found in office towers and science labs. Today, many homes sport not one but several computers, and people tapping happily on the keys of their laptops can be seen in restaurants, university lecture halls, airplanes, and even vacationing on a Caribbean beach. And North America is going "on-line" at the rate of thousands of new subscribers per day.

Although the sales hype works hard to convince people that the technology they bought six months ago is already obsolete, the truth is, many people don't need, and — more importantly to you — don't want all the fancy bells and whistles. Even an XT computer works just fine for anyone who is doing basic word processing and perhaps balancing their check book. Sure their friends may kid them about their "technological dinosaur," but there are thousands of people who can stand a lot of kidding from their friends because they know those friends paid ten or twenty times more for a computer system than they did.

Until recently, computer stores have been a relatively overlooked segment of the secondhand market place. "There aren't many secondhand computer stores around yet," says one Vancouver manager. But optimism is high that used computers represent a growth market — good news for anyone with the interest and technical expertise. "In the future, I believe we'll see a lot of larger scale operations: huge warehouses where people will have access to manufacturers' clear outs and demos at a huge discount. It's going to be expensive for the owners to set up, so it may be a long time before it happens. But it will happen."

So if you want to be on the front line of a new and growing market, this may be the perfect wave to surf. Here are some of the unique considerations you should know as you explore the world of secondhand computer selling.

a. Remembering the old days

There are already several generations of computer users who have no idea what an XT is and who have never heard of programs such as VoxWriter and BitFax, even though at one time these programs were considered deluxe additions to an office. But these are the kinds of equipment and programs you will be dealing with on a daily basis. It probably won't take you more than a couple of days before the importance of having someone on staff who is familiar with older machines and earlier versions of software becomes apparent.

As people bring in their machines, you'll need to check out whether they are actually in working order, clean them, possibly replace minor parts, and on top of all that, be able to assess whether making repairs will be worth the time and effort for both you and the customer.

If you've ever tried to fix a problem with a ten-year-old computer, you already know how difficult it is to find people who still know how to work on older machines. Finding someone who remembers how to run ten-year-old software is even tougher. And don't forget, this often means working without the help of manuals or other references. "Just figuring out the settings on some machines is a nightmare," says one computer technician.

b. Can you fix this for me?

The ability to repair equipment is necessary for any computer store, secondhand or not. The amount of servicing you choose to provide, however, will vary dramatically depending on your end goal. You need to ask yourself whether you are selling computers or servicing computers.

Some secondhand computer stores decide to act as a service center for older models in addition to selling product. The idea is that most people will eventually buy something and, in the meantime, the

Secondhand computer stores are a relative newcomer to the world of secondhand sales and may represent one of the best growth opportunities in the used goods marketplace.

If you run a secondhand computer store, you will need at least one person on staff who is used to the quirks and fits of working on older machines and early versions of software.

store is still making money off the repairs. Provided you have the necessary space and technical expertise, servicing can be a profitable add-on.

On the other hand, you may decide you want only to service equipment that will end up on the shelves of your store. If you do, be sure you keep in mind the market value of what you are working on. It can be all too easy to discover you've just devoted $100 worth of your technician's time on something that's only going to fetch $50.

Of course, servicing a computer that's brought in on consignment will mean you can, and should, charge the owner for repairs. While minor adjustments are commonplace, most experts advise against extensive repairs on consignment product because it tends to gobble up any profit.

Ultimately you will have to decide between only three options when it comes to computers in need of repair:

(a) Don't accept it. Maintain a strict "working product only" policy.

(b) Attach a label that clearly indicates the machine is not working and, if possible, an estimate of the cost to repair.

(c) Repair the unit as best you can.

c. Can I get my money back?

Unlike most other secondhand stores, used computer shops routinely offer some form of money-back guarantee. "It's almost impossible to test every component in a computer system," explains one dealer. "The customer needs some assurance that if we've missed a problem, they aren't going to be stuck paying for it."

Typically, the guarantee period is very short, a maximum of ten days in most cases. You may also want to consider a two-tiered return policy: cash refund or exchange in five days, store credit in the next ten days only.

d. Splitting the proceeds

Like most stores, your contract with the consignor will specify a percentage split. However, unlike most other types of consignment stores, there is frequently an upper limit to how much the store earns from a consignment sale. "If someone is consigning a near-new computer with a price tag of $1,800, it can really scare people off if they figure they're going to lose almost $600 dollars of that money," says one successful dealer who takes 30% of the selling price, to a maximum of $250. After the maximum is reached, the consignor pockets the entire balance, in this case close to an additional $350.

e. Finding product

By far the best sources are consignment from the general public and bulk purchases of distress sale goods or office upgrades. Initially, it will be difficult to find these bargains. As one dealer puts it, "This isn't the type of business where you can effectively get out there and beat the pavement to find the deals. Some of the very best deals for bulk purchases are made on the golf course because you just happened to be talking to the right person at the right time. If someone in your group mentions his or her office is upgrading its computer system, find out what it's planning to do with its existing equipment."

Naturally, as you build up your contacts and reputation, people will approach you with the inside scoop on which five-floor legal firm is planning to upgrade its entire office or which wholesaler is about have its warehouse of product liquidated to pay off mounting bills. Be patient. Eventually you will find yourself tapping into this source of supply almost without effort.

When these opportunities begin showing up on a regular basis, you may be tempted to choose only the best. As one dealer discovered, there can be a major payoff if you don't allow yourself to prejudge. "I got a call from a large corporation," he says. "It had a bunch of 'really old' computers that it wanted me to pick up. It didn't want any money for them, which was a good thing, because I was pretty sure they were going to be completely worthless. In the end I agreed to take them more for the PR than anything else." The dealer rented a truck and spent almost a day packing the goods out of the office and into his store. It turned out the computers were only a couple of years old and he sold the entire lot within a few days. Net profit? $5,000.

Auctions seldom represent a viable source of product. It's too difficult to assess what condition the units are in, and you'll often find you must sit through several hours of filing cabinets before the computers are on the block.

Encourage people to bring in newer (and therefore more expensive) models by setting an upper limit to the amount your store will take from a high-end sale.

f. Software

It may be a surprise to learn that used software is a staple for many used computer stores. Like hardware, programs are constantly being upgraded, revised, and even changed completely. While many people will, almost without thought, buy the newest version, there is an ever-growing market of people who realize they can work just fine with software that's a couple of versions old.

If you decide to include used software in your inventory, here are some pointers to keep in mind.

- Only original disks complete with all documentation and user manuals are acceptable. If you can get the original packaging, so much the better, but most times you won't be able to since most people throw it away shortly after they purchase the software.

- Some programs, especially very early ones and specially priced student versions, are *not* transferable. This will be indicated in the documentation. Under no circumstances should you accept non-transferable programs.

Keep a list handy of non-transferable programs for quick reference, and add to it every time you discover a new one.

- Some stores accept a verbal assurance that consignors have deleted the programs from their own computers. A safer method is to have consignors sign a legal contract transferring title and stating all other copies they may have of the program have been deleted. This places responsibility for legal transfer on the original owners, and it becomes their choice how they handle what's done with the copy on their hard drive. We strongly recommend you have a lawyer approve the wording for this document.

g. Peripherals

Other products, known as peripherals, will help round out your store so it's one-stop-shopping for people looking for a system. "If we want to compete with the large chain stores we have to carry everything from cables to disk storage units to printer stands — even when it means buying it new," says one dealer. "People can get unpleasant, to say the least, if they buy a system from us and then find out they have to run around to a couple of other stores just to get the rest of the odds and ends they need to set it up."

Here's a jump-start list of peripherals to consider:

- Adapters/connectors
- Back supports
- Cables
- Disk storage units
- Diskettes
- Document holders
- Dust covers and blasters
- Monitor supports
- Mouse pads
- Older modems
- Power bars with surge protection
- Printer stands
- Screen wipes
- Telephone cables and jacks (for Internet and fax/modem users)
- Wrist rests

This list should in no way be considered complete. As you choose among the endless number of items you could stock, you will need to judge conditions in your own location. Your customers are ultimately the best source of information about which items you should carry and which are to be avoided as shelf hogs.

Don't forget to stock the 5.25" and low density 3.5" floppy disks many older systems require.

5
Sporting goods

Ask any parent with sports-minded children and you'll likely hear the same horror story: sports cost big dollars. If the kids aren't outgrowing their equipment, they've decided last year's sport is a bore and have moved on to a different one. Two years ago it was hockey or nothing, last year was skiing, and this year everyone knows the only really "cool" activity is martial arts.

"I like to see kids play the sports they're interested in," says one sporting goods dealer. "Many young parents simply couldn't afford the equipment if they had to buy everything new." Another dealer agrees and says she often sees equipment recycled several times as parents bring product back to trade in on the next phase of interest or the next size uniform.

Here are some pointers to help you score a winning goal in the world of used sporting goods.

a. Augment consignment with small-ticket accessories

Most used sports equipment stores are primarily consignment augmented by a few small-ticket accessories such as hockey pucks, golf tees, and bicycle locks offered new. Says one dealer, "People may not want to pay full price for a brand new pair of skates, but they'll happily spring for a pair of brand new laces."

Don't expect to make much on these extras, as you will be competing against the sports mega stores that can buy in bulk at very low prices. However, you'll be able to add a bit more to your bottom line, and the goodwill you build up will pay off in the long run.

b. *Repairing doesn't pay*

Broken and very heavily used (less flatteringly described as worn-out) equipment does not sell. It may be tempting to think you can increase profits by repairing this equipment, but give it careful consideration before you open a shop in the back quarter.

Repair areas take up space, and if space is at a premium, you need to be earning a lot of money from mechanical services. To be cost effective, you will also need to stock a variety of small items such as screws, chains, tape — the list goes on.

But the biggest deterrent is that unless you own the stock outright, you may spend hours repairing a piece of equipment and then never have the opportunity to sell it at all. As one multi-store dealer points out, "Why spend a couple of hours and $10 or $20 in parts fixing someone's bike when they might decide to take it back a week or two later?" If you do provide repair services, make sure to clarify you expect consignors to pay any charges should they decide to remove the product before it sells.

Some services will make more sense than others. For example, many dealers offer skate sharpening for a small surcharge. Even if consignors ultimately decide they can live with the same size boot for another year, blade sharpening is a regular cost for any skater.

c. *Team sports*

Team sports require lots of equipment and this can mean lots of customers for you every year. Get in touch with the local amateur sports associations and let them know you are in business. A small ad in their newsletters costs very little, but will let people know they can find inexpensive, good quality equipment right in their neighborhood. Word generally spreads like lightning: the association people tell the coaches who tell the parents who tell other parents. In no time, they've built a network of sports enthusiasts who will be outgrowing and changing their equipment for the next six or seven years.

Local teams like to support local businesses. Build a reputation as a supplier of inexpensive, quality used sports equipment, and moms and dads will happily bring their business to your store over an impersonal, expensive sports mega store.

d. Exercise equipment

Exercise equipment is generally a slow mover. Some dealers speculate it's because many people prefer to work out at a gym, others suggest it's because most athletes want to get out and actually play their sport rather than work out on standing equipment.

Whatever the reason, exercise equipment takes up a lot of valuable floor space. Many stores do not carry more than a couple of pieces (perhaps a stationary bike and one rowing machine), and some don't accept exercise equipment at all. If you have limited space, consider the cost of holding a bulky item that may take up to a year to sell. No matter how good the selling price is, it may cost you too much money when you compare it to the number of pairs of skis you could move out of the same space during that time.

Exercise equipment tends to be a slow mover but will usually sell best during the winter months when rain and snow keep people indoors. And don't forget the "expanding holiday waistline" syndrome which hits most people somewhere in early January. This can be a good time to do some selective advertising to move your stock.

If you do have the floor space available, you'll need to watch current trends closely. People who use exercise equipment change their loyalties rapidly. The mini trampolines and rowing machines which were so popular in the early 1990s became an almost forgotten memory by the middle of the decade. Find out what the hot items are before you stock up.

e. Changing seasonal displays

The rule of thumb is to begin changing seasonal displays during the month prior to the next season. If the skiing season runs until April, begin weeding out the skis and snowboards in early March.

Many sporting goods stores run on basically a two season year. Here are some seasonal breakdowns of popular sports equipment.

Spring/summer:
- Baseball
- Bikes
- Camping
- Golf
- Lacrosse
- Roller blades (in-line skates)
- Tennis
- Volleyball
- Water skiing

Fall/winter:
- Figure skating
- Football
- Hockey
- Skiing
- Snowboarding
- Soccer

This is a broad outline of seasonal sports only. Naturally, there will be many differences depending on the area in which your business is located and what sports are popular — and practical — there. For example, hockey is popular almost year-round in many areas of Canada, while camping and golf enjoy 12 month popularity in the warmth and dry atmosphere of the south central United States.

f. Setting the price

If sports equipment is in good condition, you can initially put it on the floor with a price tag somewhere between 50% and 75% of the cost of new. The season, as well as "fad factors," will influence the percentage you start at almost as much as the condition of the item. If it's a trendy, new skiing gadget and the local downhill run opens in two weeks, you stand a good chance of getting a higher percentage in almost no time. However, if you're just digging out of the first snowfall of the year, don't expect to get very much for the brand new mountain bike you just accepted.

The most common discount rate in the sporting goods trade is 10% either every week or every two weeks. This is known as a Dutch auction and is explained in more detail in chapter 17. Once an item reaches zero, most store owners feel it has taken up floor space for long enough that they now own the item. At this point, it may be worth your while to put a few hours into minor repairs and store it until next year's season opens.

Be sure you specify who owns the equipment once the ticket price has dropped to zero. If you own the item, you are free to trash it, recycle it, or sell it.

6
Can you? Should you? Self-assessment

a. There are risks

No one will tell you there aren't risks involved in starting any business. You need to know what they are so you can plan your way around them.

By far the biggest risk for most starting businesses is a lack of competence and managerial experience. This lack of competence shows up in such things as:

- Poor planning
- Inadequate market analysis
- Lack of proper marketing and/or advertising
- Poor start-up timing
- Failure to anticipate the competition
- Unanticipated costs
- Shortage of working capital
- Failure to keep proper financial records
- Unexpected business problems for which the owner is not trained or prepared to cope
- Failure to stay familiar with trends in the business

Once you identify a risk and create your solution, you can stop worrying about it and forge ahead.

- Inadequate inventory control, such as marking down over-stocked inventory in order to move it
- Poor control of credit extended to customers

b. Aids to success

1. Time management

Time management will be crucial to the success of your business right from the start. If setting priorities isn't your strong suit, you can rely on some tested systems. Walk into any office stationery shop and you will find a selection of calendars, diaries, and time-management systems for sale. All are designed to help you get and stay organized.

If you are already comfortable on a computer, there are some excellent systems available that offer calendars, memo capability, and extensive list-making facilities. Day sheets and plans can be printed for your convenience. One of the good things about computerized systems is that they don't let you forget. Once you enter an item on your "things to do" list, the computer will automatically carry the item forward until you indicate that it is done.

For a detailed discussion on time management, see *Practical Time Management,* another title in the Self-Counsel Series.

2. Be willing to work hard

One characteristic that is absolutely essential to run a secondhand store, or any business for that matter, is the willingness to work hard. Without that in a small business, you are almost certainly doomed since you have the sole responsibility for the ultimate success or failure of your business.

If you do work hard you should achieve success. That success is measured not only in having a profitable business, but also in the rewards such as being satisfied with your working environment, being your own boss, and having pride in company ownership.

3. Set goals

It is crucial that you learn to set goals for your business. Without them you won't know where you are going, what to expect, or how to organize your time or resources. This is your business. If you don't set goals, no one else will, and nothing will get accomplished.

Persevere. Eliminate the words *can't* and *impossible* from your vocabulary.

4. Be service oriented

Not everyone is suited to dealing with the public. You've no doubt been in a store where this is immediately obvious. To succeed in a retail secondhand business, you must be service oriented. If you are not interested in dealing with people and their likes and dislikes, find another line of work. Customers will come into your store to spend money, to be well treated, and to be made to feel important, no matter what the size of the purchase.

Spending money, regardless of the item, takes a decision on the part of the buyer. The decision may be impulsive or well thought out. No matter. The buyer wants acknowledgment for that decision and attention for making the choice to buy from you.

When you consider the amount of money a satisfied, loyal customer can bring to your business over a period of years, the minutes you spend with that customer take on new meaning and value.

c. Self-assessment

What is it that makes one person succeed while another fails? While there is no stereotype of a successful business person, certain common characteristics can be found in those who succeed.

For example, they are invariably hard-working, determined, resourceful, and capable of honest self-appraisal.

Starting your own business is risky, and you need to be clear on whether it is the best choice for you. You may love putting on yard sales as a hobby, but turning your love into a business is a very different venture. Examining both your strengths and your weaknesses gives you the chance to remedy the factors that may impede your success. If you don't manage time well, don't like to work alone, and dislike making decisions, starting your own business may not be for you unless you are willing to work on your shortcomings. You don't have to be perfect, but you do need to recognize and acknowledge your abilities and weaknesses before investing time and money.

To aid you in your self-analysis, Worksheet #1 outlines some characteristics for success and asks you to evaluate yourself against them. Answer the questions honestly to determine how many success characteristics you already have.

This test will not definitively tell you what you should do, but it can help you engage in honest self-appraisal. You are capable of capitalizing on your strengths and compensating for your weaknesses as long as you know what they are and if your passion to succeed is powerful enough.

If your tally doesn't look strong, don't give up. Instead, consider taking on a partner who is stronger in the areas where you are weakest.

Worksheet #1
SELF-ASSESSMENT TEST

Check the appropriate column for each of the following statements.
(N = Never; M = Most of the time; A = Always)

		N	M	A
1.	I am a self-starter.	___	___	___
2.	I am usually positive and optimistic.	___	___	___
3.	I easily accept personal responsibility.	___	___	___
4.	I have no problem working alone.	___	___	___
5.	I am competitive.	___	___	___
6.	I commit strongly.	___	___	___
7.	I am flexible.	___	___	___
8.	I am self-confident.	___	___	___
9.	I relate well to other people.	___	___	___
10.	I am a goal setter.	___	___	___
11.	I am a creative problem solver.	___	___	___
12.	I like to plan.	___	___	___
13.	I am a decision maker.	___	___	___
14.	I enjoy working hard.	___	___	___
15.	I can tolerate risk.	___	___	___
16.	I seldom procrastinate.	___	___	___
17.	I am innovative.	___	___	___
18.	I handle stress well.	___	___	___
19.	I am independent by nature.	___	___	___
20.	I am a logical thinker.	___	___	___
21.	I am persistent.	___	___	___
22.	I communicate well with others.	___	___	___
23.	I manage my time well.	___	___	___
24.	I have plenty of common sense.	___	___	___
25.	I have the ability to think objectively.	___	___	___
26.	I am in good health.	___	___	___
27.	I like to learn new things.	___	___	___
28.	I am realistic.	___	___	___
29.	I can take criticism.	___	___	___
30.	I am ambitious.	___	___	___

Now determine your score. Should you start your own business? Give yourself one point for each Always and Most of the time answer; zero for each Never answer. If you scored —

30	You should be running General Motors.
26 – 29	You've got what it takes.
21 – 25	You'll do just fine.
16 – 20	Be sure you answered Always or Most of the time to numbers 14 and 27.
15 or below	Questionable.

Part II
Getting started

7

To build or buy a business?

As this book points out, starting a secondhand business from scratch requires perseverance and stamina to work out thousands of details. Buying an existing store or purchasing a franchise system are two shortcuts. Before talking about the advantages of buying a business or franchise and what is entailed, here are some of the reasons you may choose not to go that route.

a. Advantages to starting your own business

Starting your own business requires a lot less cash. You can start tiny and grow a business. If you are strapped for cash, purchasing an existing business may be out of the question.

Starting your own business means you can customize it. You don't want to open until noon? Fine. When you are starting from scratch, you don't have existing customers who already have a set of expectations that you might want to change.

You are also able to grow with the business. Running a going concern with employees to be paid, taxes due, inventory to purchase, and sales targets to meet all on the first day can be intimidating if you don't have much business experience. Starting tiny gives you time to build a solid foundation in purchasing and sales before you have to deal with your first tax return or employees.

Starting your own business also means you are not buying other people's problems and bad decisions. You make decisions on your own and learn from the results.

Chapters 8 and 9 discuss starting your own business on a small-scale — from your home — while chapter 10 looks at how to choose a location, an important issue if you plan to build your own business.

b. Advantages to buying an existing business

On the other hand, purchasing an existing secondhand business allows you to skip the myriad of details every start-up business contends with, and requires energy and cash to accomplish. Your letterhead is done, your phone is installed, the carpet is laid, the form of the organization has been decided, and customers have already been lured to your store. All you have to do is decide how you want to change things.

You also don't have to be quite as creative to buy a business as to start one. Especially if the business is successful, you also purchase the ideas that made the business a success in the first place. These might be the wonderful location, the great marketing plan, or sources of product. These details can often be the most valuable part of a business.

When you buy an existing business, you know what you are getting. You can see how the business is doing. It isn't some theoretical, abstract idea that may or may not be viable.

You'll experience less stress. Starting from scratch has risks that an established business has already dealt with. For instance, with an established store you can see how well the location works and what its problems are (e.g., parking, visibility). You don't have to make those stress-producing decisions and hold your breath to see how they are going to work out.

Especially if the business has knowledgeable employees, you can sometimes do well without knowing as much about the day-to-day operations as you would need to know before starting a business from the ground up. You can depend on your employees as you learn on the job.

And finally, buying an existing business saves time. As a very general rule, buying a business cuts about one to two years off of the growing process. This is the time it takes to carefully fill a store with saleable inventory, find and develop a location, get all the legal formalities done, and have your marketing plan begin to yield consistent results.

c. How to find a good opportunity

Many people erroneously believe that if an existing business is for sale, it must either be a package of problems or grossly over-priced. Actually, there are many good businesses for sale every day at reasonable or even favorable prices. After all, one of the reasons many people go into business is to develop a valuable asset that can be sold, providing them with lifetime financial independence and security. There are also many highly motivated sellers who will accept surprising terms just to escape, but their attitudes toward their businesses do not necessarily mean the businesses are "bad"; often it's simply bad management or poor promotion and the business itself is very revivable.

Look for:
- Advertised businesses. Your city newspaper has many businesses advertised for sale every day.
- Business brokers. In the newspaper and Yellow Pages you can find ads placed by business brokers. It will be difficult to find creatively financed opportunities through brokers, if for no other reason than the obstacle of the broker's commission, but it does happen. Also, a few hours with brokers will give you a quick crash course in what's available as well as familiarizing you with typical prices and terms.
- Business owners. Conduct a letter campaign directly to all the secondhand store owners in the geographic area you're interested in using lists compiled from the Yellow Pages.
- Franchises. There are several franchises available for secondhand goods which advertise and attend "business opportunities" shows. See Appendix 2 for a list of some of these franchises.

d. Finding and using hidden worth

Once you begin to investigate specific businesses you would consider purchasing, your biggest objective should be to discover "hidden worth" in that business.

The owner who is very close to his or her business, and perhaps tired of it, bored with it, or frustrated by it, can develop blind spots

The biggest single reason for buying an existing business, particularly a troubled one, from a highly motivated seller is seller financing (where the seller lends the buyer money, rather than the buyer borrowing from a financial institution). You can often buy a business from its owner with little or no money down and very favorable financing.

about it. He or she will often miss seeing opportunities that are obvious to a fresh, enthusiastic outsider. These blind spots translate into hidden worth for those who can see past them. In the second-hand business there are typically two common forms of hidden worth: cash-convertible assets and reorganization.

1. Cash-convertible assets

Dust-covered inventories and other equipment might be sold. You would be surprised what accumulates in the dark corners of second-hand stores: complete printing presses, wood working equipment, and valuable electronic equipment, to name just a few items that have been uncovered. Many businesses are full of idle assets just waiting to be converted to cash.

Unfortunately, inventory value in a secondhand business is hard to judge. Try to price every item to get an estimate of the liquidation value of the inventory you are buying. This requires you have a fair idea of the secondhand value of a wide range of product. You could also hire a secondhand dealer as a consultant to give you an estimate. If there are antiques that appear to be undervalued or not well merchandised, you may be able to recoup some of your investment quickly. One store purchaser sold a lamp to a buyer he knew (within hours of buying the store) and recovered 10% of the purchase price of the store.

Any part of the price based on the value of the inventory will be the subject of long and painful negotiations as the seller tries to get full retail price and the buyer tries to get the lowest wholesale price.

Many store owners will state that the price is x dollars plus inventory. This is not a reasonable method to value the business since you effectively pay for the inventory twice. The price for an existing business assumes it has inventory to sell. If there is no salable inventory, it is not an existing business.

2. Reorganization

If a business has, say, $10,000 a month of debt it must pay back, and the new owner re-negotiates all the payment schedules with vendors and creditors to reduce monthly payments to $5,000, the new owner has created $5,000 extra cash each month. This is the equivalent of $60,000 virtually out of thin air!

3. Analyzing a business

Here are the issues you need to consider and analyze in order to reveal potential hidden worth:

(a) Length of time the business has been for sale.

(b) Lowest all-cash price the seller will accept. This is important to know because even though you may have no intention of paying cash, you'll know the true lowest acceptable price. If you start out discussing seller financing, the seller instantly jacks up the price — often outrageously and always arbitrarily — to compensate for waiting for the money. But if you get the lowest acceptable price as the starting point, you can then work up in your negotiations and exercise control over the process.

(c) Seller's motivation for selling.

(d) Last month's sales, costs, and profits. Of course, you'll consider the overall financial condition, the annual past performance, and even future projections of the business, but you'll be paying your bills with the current numbers, so they deserve careful analysis.

(e) Tax situation of the business. If taxes are not all paid up, you need to know. More importantly, you need to explore the reasons why they aren't.

(f) Legal structure of the business — sole proprietorship, partnership, or corporation? You need to be sure the seller has the unencumbered right to sell the business. Divorces have forced the sale of many businesses and many a potential purchaser has found they are dealing with not just the owner but a bitter spouse as well. Your lawyer can help here.

(g) Historical documents. Get three to five years of tax records, financial statements, inventory records, customer lists, etc., and look for trends, changes, oddities to question, problems to correct, and opportunities on which to capitalize.

(h) The competition. Ask about and thoroughly investigate the competition. NEVER buy a business without fully researching the competition.

(i) Debt structure of the business. Who is owed what? Are essential vendors owed money? Who can be negotiated with? If there are 60-day, 90-day, or even older accounts payable, they can often be converted to long-term notes with very low debt service or discounted out for immediate cash payment by a new owner.

(j)   After presenting your qualifications to the seller, ask: Why do you think this would be a good business for me to buy and operate? This question is important for two reasons. First, you may learn something from the resulting comments. Second, it gets the seller into the mode of selling you. At the same time, the seller is convincing himself or herself that you are the right person for the business, which will make your negotiations easier.

(k)   Ask the seller: If you kept this business and somehow got a megabucks windfall, how would you invest it to build up this business? Again, you may learn something useful. Also, the seller is giving you the argument you'll later use to minimize the down payment.

(l)   Customer/collectors list. Go through the list one by one and discuss what each individual might be looking for, how long ago they were contacted, and whether they have bought goods before.

(m) Seller's personal financial and tax situation. Discuss this as best you can. You need to get a feel for his or her true cash needs.

(n)   Any initial and on-going assistance needed from the seller.

e. How to secure and satisfy the seller

By asking smart questions, based on the points of consideration listed above, hopefully you'll have uncovered enough hidden worth to make the business appealing. Your next step is to make a purchase offer of an amount reasonably close to the seller's stipulated lowest acceptable price. Ideally, you are willing to pay even a little more than asking price in order to get your terms.

Here are the three basic ingredients that make a seller-financing deal work:

(a)   Prove to the seller that he or she won't get a cash offer from anybody else.

From your previous contacts with business brokers and the information you gathered from them, you should be able to compile a case against the chances of the seller getting a cash offer: x number of secondhand businesses have sold in the past year, and y of those were substantially or wholly seller financed; the average selling price was only a, which was b% lower than the average asking price; and there are c number of stores that have been listed for sale longer than 12 months.

(b) As much tangible and intangible security as possible, to allay seller's fears of not being paid.

When it comes to providing the seller with security, you can give your corporate guarantee, if you are incorporated, and/or your personal guarantee, assign collateral to the business, get a co-signer with a strong financial statement to guarantee part or all of the amount, or some combination of these things. You can also offer to get "key man" life insurance for the amount of the financing, with the seller as the beneficiary, to protect him or her in case of your death.

(c) Other concessions that have cash value to the seller but installment cost to you.

Other concessions to the seller can include a continuation of his or her life insurance or health insurance, continued use of the company van or truck, office services such as telephone answering, and possibly consulting fees for some period. Many retirees want to know they are welcome to spend some time at the store to ease the transition. Although this can create problems as you make changes to their baby, the extra information and help may be exactly what you and the out-going owner both need.

There really are no set rules about negotiating deals. Perception is reality. It is the perception of the buyer and seller that determines what is and what is not a good deal.

f. Franchises

Franchises are relatively new for the secondhand scene but are growing phenomenally well. In general, franchises are supposed to provide you, the franchisee, with a systematic plan for success that has been tried and revised to the point where it is almost foolproof.

The classic come-on is that the franchiser will train you how to run your business, possibly find a great location for you, set up your systems and give you on-going marketing support. Name recognition plays a big part in some of the franchiser's spiel. How can you lose with a huge organization behind you? However, pick the wrong franchise and you can lose faster and more heavily than by starting out on your own.

On the other hand, a good franchise can be an invaluable experienced partner. Statistics show that generally franchises do better than independent entrepreneurs. Many experienced business people opt for franchises because they can concentrate on keeping sales up rather than figuring out how to get their business off the ground.

Franchises are not for everyone. You must carefully weigh the advantages and disadvantages with an eye to your own view of how your business will run. Do not go into a franchise without considering the alternatives of buying or starting your own company. If nothing else, the research you do will prepare you better for evaluating a franchise.

1. Advantages

(a) A proven concept

Decisions about the kind of customers you will go after, how you will go after them, what your image should be, and what products you will sell should already be fleshed out. Even your decor may be mandated.

People are surprisingly candid about what kind of business they run, and you should be able to get to the truth with a little persistence.

(b) Support

The franchise should have a thoroughly proven system with no bugs. Everything should be specified. You should receive assistance with anything from telephones, financing, location selection, staff selection and training to computers. The biggest help should be in marketing.

(c) Higher sales volume

Right from the beginning, you should be able to make higher sales as part of the franchise team. Make a comparison between what you would get on your own with what the franchise is promising you. Do not take their word for it. Many times franchises oversell their ability to earn you extra money. The best antidote to being oversold is to talk to as many franchisees as possible and also to independent owners.

(d) Avoidance of the set-up phase

In certain circumstances, the franchise will give you a turnkey operation. That is, all you have to do is turn the front door key the first morning and you are in business. You will pay more for this kind of operation, but you will avoid the headache and frustration of setting up everything yourself. If the turnkey operation is one you will be taking over from an existing franchise, find out exactly why it is selling out to you.

(e) Financing

Some franchisers will provide financing. Even if they do not, banks may look a little more favorably on your application for funding if you have a big name franchise behind you. Some franchisers have special relationships with banks that make it a little easier to obtain credit. You must still qualify for the money you borrow, but the bank is already familiar with how the franchiser operates and you do not have to educate the loans officer. If the franchise has a good record, you will be way ahead. If it does not, the loans officer may tell you so.

(f) Cost savings

Most franchises can save you money on some of the costs you would normally have to pay, such as inventory purchases, insurance, or employee benefits. As a franchisee, you may even get a break on your advertising rates through some form of shared advertising arrangement with the franchiser.

2. Disadvantages

(a) High cost

In addition to a franchise fee there is usually a royalty that is paid monthly or quarterly to the franchiser. The royalty fees are normally a percentage of your total sales and must be paid whether you make a profit or not. In effect you are paying an ongoing rental fee for the use of the franchiser's concepts and name. These fees can be quite steep and the franchise royalty could easily turn your modestly profitable store into a losing one.

Despite statistics about franchises having a higher rate of success, it may be that only some of the success is due to the "proven concept" explanation. One of the lopsided statistics in favor of a franchise is that of natural selection. If you have enough money for the franchise fees, and the capital the franchisers feel is required to get you through the first year, you certainly have avoided the major pitfall of under-capitalization.

(b) Advertising fees

In addition to royalty fees, you may be required to contribute a substantial amount to a national or regional advertising fund. Unfortunately, much of this money may go toward name recognition ads. Although this will help you, the franchiser benefits tremendously also. Many of the ads work just as well as a promotion for the franchiser selling their franchises. Until you reach the point where you have opened several stores in the region, more direct targeting of your potential customers may be a better use of advertising dollars.

(c) Limits on entrepreneurship

Franchises work best for those people who have good business skills but lack the flair or verve to be entrepreneurs with all the risk-taking that it entails. Managers and administrators can make very good franchise candidates, but for entrepreneurs, franchises can sometimes be a disaster.

A careful assessment of your own desires and characteristics can head off trouble if you are considering a franchise.

Typically, in the beginning a franchisee will welcome the franchiser's support and advice, and will assume the franchiser's way of doing things is best. As a year or two passes and the franchisee learns the business, he or she may begin to chafe under restrictions made by a faraway head office that does not know the local business climate. Or the franchisee may see opportunities to add products or different ways of doing business that the franchiser strictly forbids because it does not fit in with the image the franchiser has built.

(d) It is harder to change your mind

As an independent, if you discover you hate your business after a year, you can close up shop and cut your losses. With a franchise, you may be able to shut the doors, but the cash drain is likely to go on and on. Getting out of the franchise contract can be very difficult.

3. Before buying a franchise

By far the most frequent complaint about franchises is that the franchiser fails to fulfill its promises. To avoid this, work through the following steps.

(a) Speak to other franchise owners

Don't rely on the list of franchise owners supplied by the franchiser. Speak to other franchise owners to find out about the franchise, and find several people in different areas who will talk candidly about the franchiser with you. Not everything said will be complimentary. Do not buy a franchise until you have done this.

(b) References

In addition to the current owners (and past owners if you can find them), contact as many references as you can. Have the banks which the franchise works with seen mostly failures or successes? What kinds of problems have there been? Even their printer may tell you whether they pay on time or whether they always seem to be strapped for cash.

(c) Consider buying an existing franchise

Some franchisees may want to sell their franchise because of illness or changed circumstances. The franchiser will have some idea who is trying to sell. Be sure to ask about transfer fees, which may be substantial. The advantage is that much of the risk will be gone. You will know exactly what you are getting.

(d) Hire a lawyer

Definitely engage a lawyer if you are contemplating buying a franchise. The contracts supplied by the franchiser will be lengthy and cover all kinds of contingencies. This is where your rights and obligations are spelled out. Forget what the salespeople told you. Your lawyer will give you the final word on what is required of you.

(e) Read everything you can

Libraries and government offices are full of books and pamphlets that can tell you about franchises. For more information about franchising, see *Franchising in the U.S.* or *Franchising in Canada*, published by Self-Counsel Press.

(f) Heed warning signs

The flash that some franchisers put on is meant to dazzle you. Wear your darkest glasses. If your common sense says this is a get-rich-quick scheme, pay attention. If you are going to be the first one ever to be offered this wonderful opportunity, fly the coop and keep your feathers.

(g) Negotiate

Everything is open for negotiation. Be shameless in playing one franchise off against another. Can you get rid of the advertising contribution? How about for the first year? Can you get in with no franchise fee or have it financed over a very long time at a very low interest rate? Can the franchise fee be put in trust until the franchiser has completed specific things? You have nothing to lose by attempting to negotiate, so give it your best effort.

Ignore the franchiser's polished approach and friendly helpful attitude. It is part of the sales effort. Once you have signed, you may

Since there are no perfect franchises, the idea is to learn about the franchiser's shortcomings and see if you can live with them.

never see these sales representatives again. Do not be afraid to push them very, very hard.

Whether you are buying a business, starting your own or contemplating a franchise, calling some of the major franchise dealers is great way to generate good ideas. A list is supplied in Appendix 2.

8

Starting small and dreaming big

The secondhand business is tailor-made to be started part-time or full-time in your home. If you have ever sold anything through the classified section of the newspaper or run your own garage sale, you've already started.

With tight financial times, selling secondhand from one's home is not a foreign concept to most people anymore. Garage sales (discussed in greater detail in chapter 9) are so common that you already have a huge pool of customers who are used to trooping through someone's home to buy goods. In addition, the concept of reduce, reuse, and recycle is drawing in people who would never have considered secondhand goods in the past.

Many secondhand businesses were started and run from home for years before the owner finally ran out of space or wanted to expand. Most home starts concentrate on smaller items because space is a premium, but, for example, if you live on a ranch, there is no reason you can't sell tractors.

Although a separate business telephone line is one of the first things you should do for yourself once you are under way, you can start with your existing phone line: no extra expenses to pay, and people will not be surprised by your use of a home number. In fact, if you are advertising in one of the many papers around the continent that cater to people buying secondhand goods, a personal phone allows you to advertise your goods for free. Usually you have to pay an advertising fee if the phone number is for a business.

Depending on what you are selling, you probably will not need a truck to get started. Your car may do just fine for deliveries and hunting for new products to sell. With a storefront, the sales volume you must do to stay in business usually requires that you have a truck or van.

Here are some of the other advantages of starting from your home on a part-time basis.

a. Advantages of working at home

1. Low risk

The worst that can happen is that you get stuck with a few pieces of inventory you aren't able to sell. Unless you are very imprudent, you can't lose more than a few hundred dollars if you decide this business isn't for you.

2. You can try it to see if you like it

Every business has some surprises in store for new owners. You may find you are allergic to dusty things or you hate negotiating over every little lamp or toy. By starting part-time from your home you don't have to commit yourself to months of work beforehand or to a large financial burden only to find that this business isn't anything like you thought it would be.

3. Control

You can regulate the amount of business you are willing to take on. Christmas bills coming? Pump up your business. Want to take some time-consuming courses? Stop your advertising. No one will tell you what you have to do.

4. The education is free

Part of the payoff in the secondhand business is the excitement about all the diverse things you learn. You don't have to have a storefront to talk to customers who will tell you all about the things they bring you. Secondhand dealers tend to become historians and storytellers.

5. Wear what you want

When you work at home, you can dress almost any way you want. As you are selling secondhand goods, your clients are not likely to expect you to show up in a three-piece suit, so right away your style of dressing will be more casual. Some people disagree, and promote dressing up for working at home. They feel you should dress like you're working so you know you *are* working. There is no right or wrong way. If psychologically you feel better dressing more formally, go for it. All that really matters is for you to wear what you are most comfortable in.

6. *No commuting*

Get up in the morning and you're at work. This saves time, which in this era is just as valuable as money. It also cuts gasoline bills considerably. There's no time wasted in traffic and when you're through with work, you're home.

7. *You can start your business at home while still employed in a conventional job*

You can run a secondhand business on a small scale from your home and earn the extra income without losing your major source of income or quitting a profession you have built over a long time.

8. *Close to children*

Many people who still have children at home like being able to work and be around their kids.

9. *Control your work hours*

You're the boss. You can work when you want. The decision to put in extra hours or take it easy is ultimately up to you. Start at 5 a.m., take a nap later, and go back to work after dinner. Or work non-stop from 10 a.m. until 5 p.m.

If your Uncle Mort offers you a full-time position as a barkeep on the beach in the Caribbean for the winter, go for it and pick up your business when you get back. (Your business will suffer, but it is your choice. Who knows, you might be able to train your customers that you will always be closed in the month of February.)

10. *Relaxed atmosphere*

Even when you are your own boss, if you set up your business away from home, a more formal atmosphere is maintained. At home, an entrepreneur can break into song without bothering an employee or a secretary in the office down the hall. People are more comfortable in their own homes. There's less stress.

11. Better for your health

People who work out of their own homes are able to maintain healthier eating habits. It takes a special trip to visit a fast-food restaurant, but it is only a 40-foot walk to the refrigerator for a salad or fresh fruit.

People don't usually have exercise equipment both at home and in the office. But when home and office are combined, the equipment is ready to be used anytime. A routine break can turn into an exercise break, thereby giving the home-based worker an energy boost.

12. Tax write-offs

If you are operating your business from your home, you will be able to deduct a portion of your home expenses as business expenses. Chapter 24 discusses in more detail the tax advantages to having a home-based business.

13. Low start-up cost and overhead

No rent, lease, or contract payments for business space is required. If you have an area you can set aside, you're in business. Just start by purchasing something and trying to sell it.

14. Save on office equipment and supplies

You may already have some equipment and furniture that can be used to set up a home office. Your daughter's desk that is no longer being used because she graduated and left home, personal computers, answering machines, fax machines, copiers, and cordless phones — all these may be gathering dust around your home. If you already own many of the supplies and equipment you need, you save money. While you could also use personal equipment suitable for a home office in a retail store, it might look out of place.

Running a business from home may not work for everyone. What some people consider to be advantages may prove to be distractions for others who work better in a business setting.

b. Disadvantages of working at home

1. Loss of privacy

If your home office is right in your living space, customers will see how you live when they come to your office. They can see a house in need of repair, a lawn that needs trimming, carpet that needs replacing. There are no illusions.

Theft of your personal belongings is another concern: for further discussion, continue reading this chapter and also refer to chapter 9.

2. Clutter

Running a secondhand business means clutter. Inventory moves in and out, repairs have to be made, and customers come over to dig around. The work area will never look neat for long, and without strict discipline, it can spill over into your living area.

3. Distractions

At home there are always hundreds of things you could be doing. Household chores need to be done, personal phone calls need to be answered. These and other chores can drive you crazy if you let them and can easily eat up your work day.

Friends can be your worst enemies. They feel that since you are home, you must not be working and they can call or drop by to chat. You must learn the gentle art of discouraging them firmly or nothing will get done.

4. Burn out

Separating being at home from being at work is one of the hardest things for most home-based business people to do. Since your work is always at hand, there is a tendency to always answer the phone or do just one more chore. You can literally find yourself working all the time. In fact, it can reach the point where you feel guilty not working when you are home, which is a surefire prescription for burn out, family problems, and a bankrupt business.

Setting regular work hours is helpful for some people. Setting aside a specific location for your work is helpful too. Don't answer your personal phone line while working at home and never answer your business line when you are not working. A balance is crucial to your success. Everyone needs to set aside time for recreation.

5. Being pinned down

To run most types of home-based businesses you need to be home. That's the problem. If you have a store, you can hire temporary help when you need it or you can easily hire someone full-time when you need to expand. But if you work from your home, it is difficult to have someone else around, especially if you're a private person. If you want to take a vacation, it is even worse. Who will take care of your clients? Business must go on.

6. Lack of support systems

Everyone gets discouraged sometime. If you have a store with a partner or employees, someone will share a joke and tell you not to worry. Without people around to add encouragement and act as sounding boards, working at home can leave you feeling vulnerable and isolated.

7. Neighboring problems

Depending on where your home business is and how much repair work you do, you may find your neighbors give you grief over noise or odors. And even with the correct city permits for a home-based business in your area, the parking problems *caused by* customers coming and going might irritate your neighbors to the point that they complain to city hall.

8. Family interruptions

You're deep in thought trying to solve a serious business problem. You want to get the solution down on paper or into the computer. Your spouse walks in and expects a hug. What do you do? If you're smart, you hug. The great business thought will come again. Get the hug while you can. Family interruptions are to be expected, but with proper juggling of work hours, some interruptions can be alleviated. You don't want to bar family members entirely from your work space because they are one of the advantages of working at home.

9. Lack of respect

A complaint often heard from people who work at home is that friends make comments like, "I wish I could stay at home and do nothing like you," or "Why don't you have a real job?" Some home-based entrepreneurs may have trouble being taken seriously by family, friends, prospects, and bankers. There are people who have trouble understanding you are running a serious business from your home. Most of these reactions come from people who don't really know what people who work from home actually do. Comments like, "Well, I've been working since 5 a.m., so I decided to take the afternoon off" usually get the point across without ruffling feathers.

10. Self-discipline

Any entrepreneur, especially one who works from home, has to be a self-starter. No one is going to give you a push in the morning, you have to do it yourself.

11. Lack of commitment

There is something sobering about contemplating leases and loans. Running a small part-time business from your home means you have to supply the motivation to do it. No one will force you in any way to continue. This is a procrastinator's heaven.

12. Shoparama

There are people who start small secondhand businesses in their home as an excuse to go antique shopping. Remember that selling your purchases is the true test of whether this is a business or not. You can't just use it as an excuse to buy everything you like. It may sound funny, but this can be a serious problem.

13. Theft

It is not pleasant to think that someone you invite into your home would steal from you; it is not something you would expect to have to guard against. If you run sales inside your home, be sure to hide all money, jewelry, and valuables well. Purses are tempting targets. More than one person has been the target of "gangs" of little old ladies who take anything they can lay their hands on once they are inside the house. Remember, opportunities for diversionary tactics abound when you are alone with an opening rush of people.

Always try to have a second person work with you, especially if your customers are entering your home. At the very least, put up barriers to your personal valuables.

c. Nine home-based strategies

You can't just decide to run your business from home, hang up a sign, buy an answering machine, and start earning money. It isn't quite that simple. There are some other aspects of running a business that must be taken care of.

1. Check local zoning requirements

Check your city zoning regulations to see if you can legally run a business out of your home. Depending on the size of the business you are considering, you may be barred from operating from your home.

Especially at the beginning when your business is small, you shouldn't have a problem. There are no rules that prohibit someone from occasionally selling something out of his or her home. But as you get larger, with more people coming to your door or garage, you need to know exactly what the rules are. Talk to an authority at your city hall. He or she can explain which guidelines apply to your specific situation and what you will need to do to ensure your business conforms to them.

2. Obtain permits and licenses

All cities require permits for just about everything. As you grow out of the occasional sale stage, find out what permits you need to conduct your business.

3. Buy insurance

Don't fool around with your insurance coverage. There are different policies for purely residential coverage and a combination of residential and business. If you are covered only for residential and you have a claim for fire or theft, it is pretty easy for an insurance adjuster to figure out that you are running a business. Claims for a garage full of antique lamps and gramophones will be a red flag. Your insurer might decide not to pay you for your losses.

Talk to your insurance agent and let him or her shop around for you. Some companies will not cover home-based businesses, but there are many that do. The small amount of extra cash required to cover home businesses is a small price to pay for peace of mind. Chapter 15 discusses the importance of insurance in more detail.

4. Research legal requirements

Before opening your door, find out what state/provincial and federal laws apply to your business. Ask your local small business bureau or chamber of commerce for information. There may also be a national or local association for your business. See Part III of this book for a discussion of legal requirements needed to start a business.

5. Be a self-starter

Working for yourself means freedom to do what you want. By working at home you have even more freedom. As a successful entrepreneur you have to be a self-starter. No one is going to tell you when you have to work. That is up to you, but if you don't work, you won't get paid.

6. *Establish regular working hours*

For many people, it is best to use regular working hours. That way you know when it is time to work, when it is time for a break, and when it is time to quit for the day. One nice aspect about being your own boss is that you can change your schedule when you need to. Many stay-at-home caregivers run their business by appointment so they are free to attend to errands. It is also possible to have regular hours, say Saturday between 10 a.m. and 3 p.m., and simply put a "back in five minutes" sign on the door if you have to dash out. As long as it doesn't happen too frequently, you probably won't lose customers.

7. *Be a joiner*

Join community groups and business associations. Find ones that match your personality. You can use them for making contacts, but they are also really beneficial for helping you keep your sanity.

8. *Know when to grow*

Many home-based secondhand businesses outgrow their origins within the first few years. Some people want to grow as fast as they can so they can have warehouses and storefronts. If this is your goal, plan for that growth when you draw up your business and financial plans. But plan to achieve it slowly.

9. *Know when to stay home*

Some people feel they need to expand if they are to be perceived as successful. If you do expand, make sure there is a definite need for your expansion, such as a need for warehousing, a storefront, and parking. There are significant extra expenses and time demands, and bigger risks associated with working from a commercial property. And there is not necessarily more profit. Unless you're making more money, why leave home to do the same thing you could be doing from home?

For more information on home-based businesses, you may want to refer to *Start and Run a Profitable Home-Based Business*, another title in the Self-Counsel Series.

More than 9,000 new businesses are begun every day in the United States and Canada. Many of these are home-based businesses. They can be successful and rewarding, but they take planning. They don't just happen.

9
A little bigger

Sometimes it is just not possible to run a business entirely from home. You may be already strapped for space, have students or relatives requiring quiet, or you may find the disadvantages described in the previous chapter outweigh the advantages.

Here are four methods for doing business that will allow you to enjoy some of the upsides of a home business without putting a lot of pressure on your living space. They are worth considering as a means of expansion or as a way to start the business part-time without using your home.

a. Garage, carport, or basement sales

Garage, carport, or basement sales are not complicated, but they do require time to prepare. Basically you set up a table with your goods on it, alert the customers, and sell. Here are some points to keep in mind.

1. Seasonality

Garage sales are a year-round phenomenon, but spring cleaning doubles the number of sales going on. It also brings out the largest number of customers. By late fall, most garage sales have ended and the papers only list a few moving, house, or estate sales. Naturally, the season is longer in areas where the weather is good most of the year.

There is not much you can do about the weather except prepare as best you can with cover for your goods and customers. Rain will always drown out some customers and cold will freeze you. Your choices are to set up your garage with heat, which is expensive, or stick to putting on garage sales seasonally.

2. Advertising

Advertise around your neighborhood by putting up signs and giving out handbills. Many local and major newspapers have sections devoted entirely to advertising garage sales.

Make it easy for people to find your house by putting out colored balloons along with signs at major intersections. These will help show people the easiest route to your house. Another group of balloons or an eye-catching object should mark the entrance to your sale. A four-foot high plush bunny rabbit has been used by one dealer for years.

3. Pricing

Pricing is a long and tedious task. Sellers who don't put on stickers must answer questions all day about the price. On the other hand, without a price on the item, you can charge what you think the market will bear. Just be careful you remember what you told various customers.

The other advantage to stickers is that if you run several sales per year, the prices you tried last time are still on the goods. This can do two things for you:

(a) You won't have to price them again, or

(b) You know it didn't sell at the marked price so you can try a new lower price.

4. Neighbor trouble

There is a limit to how much business you can do before you begin to run into bylaw and neighbor problems. You can't run a big sale with newspaper advertising announcing the "Saturday Extravaganza" or post big signs touting the "Big-one-day-25%-off sale at 3476 Bridal Street" very often before you attract city bylaw attention.

If you run a sale every week, neighbors may complain and the city may require you to get a license and comply with other regulations.

5. Theft

As discussed in chapter 8, it is not pleasant to think that someone you invite into your home would steal from you. Theft is not common at garage sales, but eventually you will run into it. After all, you are making a public invitation and you will get a normal cross-section of society.

If several people are working with you, keep an eye on each other. When you see goods going out the door, know which of your friends or employees sold those goods. If you don't know, find out. Big items such as couches can disappear, too. You think the person carting it out paid your friend, and your friend thinks you were paid for it. Owners have actually been known to help the thieves load up their prizes.

6. Organize beforehand

Finish putting everything out before people arrive. If you aren't distracted by trying to price stuff or move it out of boxes, you can do more selling and keep a closer eye on your goods.

7. Keep it fresh

You need new inventory to run a sale every week. Your sales will fall off if people see the same old thing at your street-side shop and you'll become just another merchant they drop in on occasionally. If you don't keep restocking, eventually all your good stuff will be sold, leaving you with only the junk which you may have to pay to have removed.

b. Consignment shops

One big advantage of reselling through other people's stores is that you can learn your particular secondhand business slowly without it taking over your house. All the goods you buy are consigned somewhere else.

You have to be fairly astute to buy secondhand goods and then resell them on consignment. Consignment means a shop owner agrees to sell your goods and split the proceeds with you for whatever they are paid. The problem is that you are selling secondhand to a crowd which expects cheap prices. On top of that, you have to give away up to 50% of the selling price to the shop owner. Most items you can sell at a profit through a consignment shop have to be very cheaply acquired.

Not that it is impossible. A ratty looking dress pulled from the bottom of a trunk might only need a little TLC to show its true worth. A lamp cheaply acquired that just needs a cleaning or a little repair might glow in the expensive setting of an antique store.

1. Start by selling

This is a chance to hone your buying and merchandising skills at little cost. You don't even have to start by buying. Have a look in your closet or around your home. You'll get an idea of which items the stores want simply by trying to sell some of your own under-utilized goods.

2. Sell to whom?

Look in the Yellow Pages for stores that take items on consignment. Check all secondhand stores. Many of these stores will tell you right up front if they do consignment. Even if a secondhand store does not normally advertise that it accepts consignment, it may do so when inventory stocks are low or if you have a unique item it could showcase in the store to attract customers.

3. Protect yourself

Try to get references on stores where you intend to leave goods. Ask the Better Business Bureau in your area for a report. Occasionally unscrupulous store owners won't pay for goods they have sold for you. If you can't get references or are too shy to ask, start small by consigning something that isn't going to hurt you too much if you lose it.

Prompt payment is essential before you give a store too many things to sell. Late payment should be a red flag about doing future business with that store again.

Get everything in writing. A complete description of the goods, serial numbers if there are any, the terms of payment, any special conditions (for instance, the minimum you will allow the store to sell it for), and a signature of a store employee.

4. What kind of profit split?

Usually there are some guidelines about how much you want for an item and how much leeway the store has in selling it. The store might, for instance, offer to split the money they sell the item for 50/50, and you might want $20 in order to earn a bit of profit. If the store puts a price of $50 on a coat, it knows it can negotiate on the

Most people who successfully make money with consignment shops look for quality or uniqueness or both to ensure sales.

67

price a bit as long as it doesn't go below $40. Of course, if the store doesn't mind cutting some of its commission, it can cut the price to $25 and still make a bit of cash.

5. *Organize*

Keep good records on where things are. The fastest way to a sure loss is to forget where you left something. A simple filing system with a note of explanation stapled to the receipt for each item will keep everything in one place.

6. *If all else fails*

You do need a plan of action for what you are going to do with an item you purchase that no one wants or that doesn't sell. Certainly trying several stores or lowering the price is a possibility. But eventually, even these options may be closed to you. Go back to section **a.** above. Have a garage sale. Alternatively, box up several things and sell it as a "surprise" package for next to nothing at a secondhand store.

c. *Flea markets and malls*

Every town in North America has a flea market at some time. Even malls have entered the act, enticing customers by having flea markets inside — a particularly popular attraction during the Christmas season.

1. *Sharing a table*

Sharing a table at a flea market alleviates a lot of problems. There is always someone to take over at your table when you need a break, and you can split any entrance fees.

The best people to share with are those who know something about your goods and can negotiate a reasonable sale price in your absence. But, unless your goods are carefully marked, don't expect your partner to do any selling for you. More than once a stand-in has sold an item for much less than the owner wanted.

Remember, no one can sell items that you bought as well as you can. You are the one who knows the history of the goods and the features that made you buy it in the first place. If you are off shopping most of the day, you won't sell much.

One of the exciting things about a flea market is the buying or trading opportunities around you. Much of this goes on before the gates are open to the public so it is a good idea to arrive early to see what is available.

2. Getting there

Unless you are dealing in antique watches, sports cards, or jewelry and live no more than two or three blocks away, you'll need your own transportation to the venue. Taxis can quickly eat your profit.

3. Theft

You really do need to have another person you can rely on at a flea market — for loading, unloading, and covering you on eating breaks — otherwise it is very difficult to protect your goods from theft. You can count on the people at your neighboring tables for some relief; after all, everyone has the same problem. But don't expect them to act as a full-time security guard for your product: they have their own to look after.

4. Location, location

The best place to set up a booth is near an entrance or an exit, as every visitor will walk by you. Near washrooms or eateries has this advantage, too, but if lineups form, your table or booth might be hidden from the wandering crowds.

Prime locations may cost a bit more and are almost always allocated on a first-come, first-serve basis. So if you want the best booth in the house, be sure to reserve early.

d. Renting space in a store

It is not uncommon to find several different antique and secondhand dealers selling goods from the same store and splitting the rent. Sometimes there is a lead tenant who is ultimately responsible for the store and who rents out space to smaller vendors.

This arrangement has many of the characteristics of running your own store without some of the headaches. Of course, there are advantages and disadvantages:

1. Advantages

The advantages of sharing space include:

- You don't have to invest large sums in stock, display cases, and other fixtures. It is possible to start with a 100 square foot (9.3 square meter) "store" and build it up a little at a time.

- Different specialties mean more variety, which tends to attract customers.

- The other tenants can sell your goods while you take a break.

- The store has a built-in security force that you couldn't match on your own. This is especially true when several vendors are in the store.

- Dealers may specialize in just a few areas but are knowledgeable about other goods. If you don't know about an item, one of your colleagues might.

- Some of your co-tenants might be customers and sources of goods for you.

- Your co-tenants are walking advertisements for you. When they're talking to a customer who is looking for a particular item, they'll know if you have it.

- There is always someone available to help you unload that awkward chest from your vehicle.

- Normally you don't have to worry about lease negotiations or leasehold improvements. When the lease is up for renewal, your holdings may be small enough that you don't even have to worry if the main tenant doesn't get a renewal. You simply pack up and leave.

    Although this certainly takes some pressure off you, the larger the number of items you have stocked, the more of a problem it tends to be. And if you have developed a good business at the location, you'll not want to give up the space. Of course, this may be entirely out of your hands, in which case you'll have little choice but to find another, new location.

2. Disadvantages

The disadvantages of sharing space include:

- Space can get tight and other peoples goods might start to encroach on your territory. Although a certain amount of cooperation is expected — after all, you will have times when a special buying opportunity overstocks you — chronic overstocking can make effective merchandising next to impossible.

- Your co-tenants might not all be honest.

- You have very little control over who cohabits with you. One of the other tenants may have an alcohol problem which might not be apparent until you have moved in and discovered you are losing customers.

- Personality conflicts take time to develop and can be a source of real grief.

10
Finding a location

For many of you, your location will be the linchpin of your marketing effort; picking the proper location will be essential to getting customers in the door. For those of you who do not depend on walk-in or drive-by traffic, your task is much easier since a wide range of locations is available to you. The trick is to find a less popular and less expensive location that is still attractive to potential clients and then use the savings to mount an effective marketing campaign.

a. Choices, choices, choices

1. Enclosed malls

When you think of malls, you probably think of a huge regional shopping mecca. But there are thousands of small malls across the continent, some with only two or three stores. Most malls will not accept secondhand stores that specialize in general goods (upscale antique stores are more acceptable), but many will accept stores selling secondhand clothes and computers. A few down-at-the-heels malls will accept any business that pays the rent, but you should evaluate these and the people they attract carefully before committing yourself.

Malls have several advantages over other types of locations, but you pay for them. Here are some of the usual benefits found by having a mall location:

(a) There is generally plentiful, free parking.

For information on what is available in your area contact a real estate office or leasing agent. You should also look through the classified sections of the newspaper and drive around areas you are interested in.

(b) Security is provided, even if it is only in the form of the mall management occasionally making the rounds.

(c) Malls are recognizable and accessible to passersby.

(d) Other businesses nearby help draw clients to you.

(e) The mall may have a program of shared advertising.

(f) Competition within the mall is often limited, so you do not have to worry about other secondhand stores. (Check your lease carefully for this important provision.)

(g) The mall management may have statistics about the demographics of the mall's customers and a very accurate walk-by count.

There are some disadvantages to locating in a mall:

(a) There are almost certainly more rules to comply with than with a stand-alone store. Many of these, such as the type and amount of insurance you must carry or the kind of leasehold improvements you must make, may cost you money.

(b) Malls normally dictate the hours you must stay open. If the mall is open late seven days a week, you must staff your store for the entire time, even though people may not shop in that mall on Sundays and late evenings.

(c) Larger malls may not let you rent if you lack an established credit history.

(d) The price per square foot is relatively high.

2. Retail street-level and small strip malls

Street-level properties in very high-rent areas are usually comparable in price with large, enclosed malls. But prices for a street location in small strip malls are more varied and much less expensive. Depending on your landlord, there are also normally fewer rules and you can set your own hours.

The disadvantages of street-level stores often include chronic parking shortages, which can have a serious effect on your business, and lack of security, especially if you have alleys and possible entry points from skylights and back doors. You may incur extra security costs for alarms, steel shutters, or security patrols.

3. Downtown versus suburban

Some highly cosmopolitan areas of large cities are not conducive to secondhand businesses. Fifth Avenue in New York, for example, is just too pricey. But suburbs and smaller cities or towns may be perfect. Take a look around.

Downtown does have a higher concentration of customers than the suburbs, but sometimes it also has more competition. Parking and accessibility can be a major headache, especially in large cities. It's also a growing trend to find downtown locations dead on Sundays and evenings, while suburban shopping areas are bustling with activity.

b. *Other considerations*

When selecting your location, consider these important points:

(a) Ask yourself if the location you are contemplating satisfies the needs of your customers. For example, if you are supplementing your business with rentals, are you where your customers will be? If you rent primarily for movie sets or plays, are you near studios or the theater district? Parking is a major consideration for everyone.

(b) Find out if the rent is competitive. Is there something cheaper in a similar neighborhood? Check with a leasing agent and survey other locations.

(c) Check the essential leasehold expenses. Essential leasehold improvements are those that add to security and visibility or improve the layout. For a basic store, they should be small. The added expense of putting steel bars on a back door can be hefty, so be sure you have a very clear idea of what it will cost.

(d) Know where your competition is located. Will customers simply cross the street and start a bidding war for certain goods that all secondhand places carry? Would you welcome the competition or not? Remember, not all secondhand stores are your competition. Many specialize and may not affect your target market at all. Sometimes having many secondhand stores in one area helps business because people have been educated to go to that particular area to shop for antiques and collectibles.

(e) Think about the general atmosphere of the neighborhood. Is the area on the way up or on the way down? How much new construction is there? Do people in the area take pride in their neighborhood and keep it clean and in good repair?

(f) Check the crime rate. Is the area a hangout for undesirables in the evenings or weekends?

(g) Find out why the location is vacant. What was there before? Why is it gone?

(h) Determine how much space you need. Stores come in every possible configuration and size. We have seen used-goods stores as small as 200 square feet (18.6 square meters). Consider your prospects for acquiring a larger space if you need it later. Perhaps the property owner would be willing to let you swap your smaller space for a larger store if one becomes vacant later.

(i) Corner sites are more valuable because there are two streams of pedestrian and/or vehicular traffic. Many of them have double the window display area, too. Count on paying more.

c. Assessing walk-in traffic

There is no easy formula for the crucial selection of a location that will bring you walk-in traffic. Be prepared to spend extra time and money researching your target location to ensure your success. Few secondhand stores survive a terrible location. The following points may help you make your decision:

(a) The most important question to ask yourself is whether the extra rent you will pay in a popular spot could be better spent on a concentrated advertising campaign. Paying big bucks for the privilege of sitting and waiting for customers who never walk in the door is not the way to go. A scintillatingly creative marketing campaign may be cheaper and better.

(b) Do a traffic count and compare the number of people going into prosperous-looking secondhand stores in other parts of town. Simply count up the number of prospective clients passing your location in a given time period. Try several different times. However, when comparing, remember that other secondhand stores might not be as prosperous as they look or they may not depend on walk-in traffic for their profit. Traffic counts also give you some basis for comparing rent you would pay in different locations. Within reason, it may be a more useful comparison than using cost per square foot or per square meter.

(c) Determine if the foot traffic is appropriate to your marketing plan. Seasonal tourists usually do not shop for bulky items, so a high traffic count in a tourist area may be useless. Likewise, an area frequented by the teenagers may yield a high traffic count and still have a low potential for sales.

(d) Use a map to chart where the competition is and the demographics of your potential customers. By explicitly mapping the competition, you will not overlook anyone. And if you map demographics, even if the numbers aren't perfect, you may learn a lot about potential market size. How many people in a subdivision or a particular office tower are really your customers? Consider that a new subdivision may be populated by first-time home owners with young families who are going to be looking for ways to economize by purchasing secondhand goods.

(e) Consider negotiating a month-to-month lease so you can try one location without a long-term commitment. Moving a secondhand store is expensive, disruptive, and time-consuming, but in the end it is cheaper than pouring rent into the wrong location.

d. Store layout

When you look for an appropriate site for your store, you should ensure it has adequate interior space for inventory, an area for an office, and possibly even a receiving and shipping area.

You should also consider the necessity of space for expansion when business improves. If you are considering expansion, the space for inventory should be more than adequate to take care of today's inventory needs as well as providing room for your growing amount of inventory as business increases.

Before you sign any lease you should spend a fair amount of time visualizing and committing to paper exactly what you think the store will look like when you are up and running. Once you have dressing rooms installed in your clothing store, will there be enough room for displaying your products? Is the roof high enough to accommodate tall cabinets or the four-poster beds you might buy? How much window frontage is there and how much of your store is visible from the street?

A worthwhile exercise is to draw a scale map of the proposed store on graph paper. Using the same scale, cut out shapes representing all the items you know you will be trying to fit in: your front counter, chair, display racks or cabinets, filing cabinet, even the dressing rooms you need to build. Everything you know you must have to make your store work should be sketched out. Now try to fit it all on your map and see how much space you have left over. This simple exercise often avoids moving the actual item three or four times as you're setting up.

e. Negotiating the lease

Great care should be taken when negotiating a lease. It could easily commit you to paying as much to the landlord as you pay to set up your secondhand store. Think about it: $1,000 a month for five years is $60,000! Your manageable $30,000 budget for a new secondhand store may become a $90,000 bombshell.

Take as much time and effort to understand the lease as you do when negotiating any of your other agreements. Read it over several times. Have your lawyer and accountant read it. Confirm every detail in the contract no matter how fussy and time consuming this may seem. The last lease we signed committed us to pay for utilities on the basis of the square footage. The measurements in the contract were wrong and we paid an excessive amount for over five years. A small item, but we'd rather have had the money than given it to the landlord.

Before you sign your lease, answer these questions:

- Do the heating and air conditioning work?

- Is there a washroom for you and your staff?

- What kind of signs are allowed? Are there restrictions on what you can put in the window? What you can put on the sidewalk? (See section **f.** below.)

- Does any pre-existing unchangeable color scheme fit with what you want? Especially in malls, you will sometimes have to use a certain color scheme.

- Can you alter the premises to your specifications?

- Is there enough electrical power to run your computers and lighting and for your display window? Are there sufficient plugs to give you flexibility when you set up your store? Before you say yes, check every switch and plug to make sure they work.

- Is there adequate room for a messy storage/work area?
- Does the roof leak? Look for water stains.
- What will your insurance premiums be like in this location? Get several quotes.
- Is your plate glass window open to the street? Is it covered by the landlord's insurance or yours?
- How is security for the building? Are there points that are easily accessible to an intruder? Where are the fire exits? Will the landlord pay to upgrade these?
- In the winter when it's dark before closing time, will your employees be safe when they walk to the bus or parking lot?
- Can any large products you've purchased be easily delivered?
- Is there enough parking for you, your staff, and customers? Is it included in the lease or is it extra?
- Do traffic patterns make this a difficult spot to get to? Divided highways and one-way streets are perfect examples of restrictions that can be a problem for your customer.
- Can your store be easily found?
- What side of the street is the space on? This might be more important than it appears to be at first glance. In North America, north sides of streets (with southern exposure) normally get a lot of sun, which can cause overheating problems in the summer and fading of goods placed in the window.
- How visible is the store to passing motorists? Can you improve this by signs or your display window?
- Are there any businesses nearby that create loud noises, foul smells, or attract undesirables?
- Is major construction going to start next door?
- Are the surrounding buildings in good repair? If they aren't, they may detract from your store.
- Is there another store or attraction close by that draws seasonal business? What will you have to do to get customers in your store at other times of the year?
- If there is little competition in the area or if your competition is not aggressive, what impact would it have on your business if it suddenly beefs up its marketing and promotional activities?

- Is there a demolition clause in the lease? Demolition clauses are a way for the landlord to terminate the lease with only a few months' notice to allow for development of the property. If the landlord wants this clause, it can be a great deal for you if you're willing to face the chance of a forced move later. Push extremely hard to have the cost of the lease reduced and use the savings to build your business when you move. If you are cash poor in the beginning, a property like this might be perfect.

f. Bylaws and similar problems

Before going too far with what seems a desirable site, make sure that all the local bylaws such as zoning restrictions, building codes, fire regulations, and similar laws will allow you to operate your store there.

1. Zoning

Zoning regulates such matters as size of structure, the portion of a lot that may have a building on it, proximity to the street, parking requirements, the use to which a building may be put, and the size and type of outdoor sign permitted. If you have any doubts, check first with your local government's planning/zoning department.

Sign ordinances should also be checked to determine if there are any restrictions on type, placement, number, and size of signs.

Make sure the information you obtained concerning bylaws and ordinances is up-to-date since changes do occur in these regulations from time to time.

2. Highways

Ask the highways department to provide information concerning its future plans for new highways or bypass routes that could severely affect the visibility and accessibility of your store.

For example, if the store is on a two-lane highway that is slated for widening to four lanes, is a divider planned for separating the two halves of the highway? If this is the case, it may make if difficult, if not impossible, for arriving or departing motorists to drive directly into or out of the property.

g. Merchants associations

Find out if there is a local merchants association. If there is, attend one or two meetings to find out the concerns of other local merchants. Meetings are also a perfect opportunity to network and find out who are the industry leaders in that area.

Part III
Business foundations

11
Professional help

When you start up your new secondhand business, you are going to need some professional help from a banker, accountant, lawyer, and possibly other specialists and consultants.

a. Banker

For most small businesses a small, local branch bank is likely to be of more help than a big city bank that handles only large accounts. You should advise your banker of your intention to start a business and keep him or her informed of your progress.

Consider your bank as not just a place to store money, but also as a possible provider of the following services:

(a) Credit references on your customers or potential customers

(b) Financial and investment advice

(c) Money to start and eventually to expand your business

(d) Check certification

(e) Safety deposit box

(f) Night depository

(g) Payroll and other accounting services

Wherever possible, try to find a bank that is close to your business, at least for daily deposit of receipts, since this will minimize the risk of losing them on the way to the bank. An outside depository that does not require a bag makes night deposits possible. If you have to pick up a bag during banking hours, you may have to close your doors while doing so, which can be inconvenient.

b. Accountant

If you do not have qualifications in accounting, you will need an accountant to at least handle your annual tax return. Tax law and tax accounting for businesses is complex. Few small business owners have the competence or the time to be knowledgeable about all of the intricacies of income tax.

An accountant can help you set up your initial accounting and control systems.

This does not mean you should not try to familiarize yourself with income tax rules and regulations. That knowledge can be helpful in the day-to-day operation of any business, but a professional adviser in this area is well worth the cost.

As well as preparing your periodic financial statements, an accountant can interpret and analyze them for you and advise on growth possibilities for your company when it is well established.

Choosing an accountant is as important as choosing your doctor or lawyer. You want someone with a good professional reputation who also makes you feel comfortable. Avoid anyone who can converse only in unintelligible accountant's jargon or who bills you for a telephone conference if you call to clarify a minor point. Look for a professional who regularly deals with and understands the needs of small businesses and is prepared to help you set up a simple system along the lines recommended in this book.

If you don't know where to start looking, ask your bank manager or a business acquaintance if he or she can recommend someone. Don't be afraid to talk to several accountants before making a choice and don't hesitate to ask about their fees. A good accountant can actually save you far more than his or her fee, but that doesn't mean you don't need to know the fee in advance.

c. Lawyer

Finally, you will probably need a lawyer since there are always some legal matters to be taken care of in starting a business. One is the legal form of your business (see chapter 13).

Other matters where legal advice is useful for a person starting and operating a small secondhand business might include issues concerning the rights of:

(a) Buyers and sellers of merchandise

(b) Landlords and tenants

(c) Creditors and debtors

(d) Employers and employees

(e) Purchasers and sellers of land and/or buildings

(f) Borrowers and lenders of money

A lawyer can also check items such as licensing requirements and rental contracts, as well as make you aware of any special governmental requirements that may exist in your area for your business.

d. Consultant

One type of consultant you will probably need is an insurance agent. Although it is doubtful you will need other consultants to start your business, you may need some special managerial or marketing consultants as your business expands.

Specialists can advise in areas such as business layout, inventory control, business organization, advertising campaigns, and many similar areas where you need special help at a particular time.

These specialists, since they are not involved in day-to-day operations as you will be, can often view your business in a more objective way and give professional advice to help you improve your profits.

Consulting services have expertise in preparing feasibility studies for new business proposals, searching out good sites, documenting loan proposals, and similar services. Beware though, consulting fees can run from reasonable to outrageous.

A word of caution about consultants: there are many who charge more than their advice is worth. Since there are no licensing, certification, or competency requirements for consultants, anyone can promote himself or herself as a consultant with the sole intention of extracting money from you.

In particular, be wary of consultants who offer to find you money for a fee based on the amount of money raised — for example, 10% of the $200,000 you need, or $20,000. A reputable lender would probably not lend money if an intermediary were involved for such an exorbitant fee.

Use a lawyer who will tell you in advance the cost of his or her service, even the cost of an initial meeting.

e. Choosing your professional advisers

Shop around when choosing your professional advisers. Bankers, accountants, and lawyers, like all business people, are in competition with each other.

Even though these professionals (particularly accountants and lawyers) are members of professional associations and must demonstrate competency in their field, there are degrees of competency, and of specialization. Do not choose the first one you visit because of a positive impression, even though that first impression can be important in your final decision.

Let each professional know you are discussing the situation with two or three others in their profession. This way you may not be charged for your short initial meeting since it may encourage you to stay with them in the long run.

Ask friends who are in business, or people you meet socially or on other business matters for recommendations.

Don't choose a professional adviser solely because you know him or her socially. Try to find a lawyer or accountant who is familiar with secondhand businesses.

If you plan to locate in a particular area, selecting a lawyer, an accountant, and a banker in that area can be preferable since they will be familiar with local conditions and will be easier to visit when necessary.

1. Be prepared for questions

Professional advisers are going to ask you questions almost from the outset. You should try to have the answers to these questions ready, even in an exploratory first meeting.

These questions will include such matters as the size of business you are thinking of starting, the organizational form of your company (proprietorship, partnership, or private limited company), how much money you can invest yourself, how much money you may have to borrow, and when you plan to start the business.

2. Cost of professionals

You will want to know how much you are going to pay for professional advice. Bankers do not normally charge for their time. Their profit is made from the interest rate they charge you for money you borrow and for the use they make of business funds you have on deposit in accounts with them.

Accountants and lawyers usually charge on an hourly basis, or alternatively charge an annual retainer fee for certain ongoing day-to-day advice, with an extra charge for matters that fall outside what is included in the retainer. In order to minimize your costs, a retainer approach is probably not a good idea unless your business is going to require a great deal of professional advice.

If your accountant is also going to produce your monthly accounts, there will likely be a flat monthly charge for doing this. Filing the annual tax return might be included in this monthly charge. Alternatively, it may be an additional annual cost.

Since accountants and lawyers do have a fairly high hourly fee, try to minimize the amount of time you use them. As much as possible, make decisions for yourself and only call on them when a matter to be resolved is critical and where proper professional help is required.

Check at the outset what the procedure is for advice. Generally, accountants and lawyers, like most business people, prefer to arrange face to face meetings with as much advance notice as possible. They generally prefer not to give advice over the telephone concerning important matters that require documentation.

12
Financing your business

A retail secondhand store is a major undertaking which will require several thousand dollars to just open the doors. Lease deposits, more inventory, licensing and other legal fees, installation charges for phones and security devices, and a host of other expenses add up quickly.

Before you can even begin looking for sources of funding for your business enterprise, you need to know how much money you will need. Not only do you need to know so you are "shopping" for money with a definite goal in mind, but your prospective financiers will want to see some realistic figures before they even consider your request. After all, they will want to know whether you will need a loan of a few thousand dollars or a few million!

Going after too little money is at least as damaging as seeking an excessive amount of money, and it's not necessarily easier to get a smaller amount than a larger one. What you want to do is to go after and get the right amount of money. To arrive at that amount, you'll need to do some financial forecasting.

a. Income and expense forecast

An income and expense forecast can be described as the operating statement you would expect to see for your business at the end of the period for which the forecast is being prepared. Generally, this period is a year. For a new business, the forecast shows what revenues and expenses you *predict* the business will have in its first year of operation. Your analysis should answer the basic question of whether you are going to make money from your enterprise.

The first figure to estimate is income or sales. Unfortunately, it is also the most uncertain. If you have already been running a home-based business, you have a solid basis for making predictions. But be conservative: it's better to underestimate than to go overboard.

Now, prepare a list of expenses, including such things as —

    (a) labor,

    (b) inventory,

    (c) depreciation,

    (d) advertising,

    (e) insurance,

    (f) utilities,

    (g) rent,

    (h) taxes,

    (i) interest on loans,

    (j) professional services, and

    (k) miscellaneous costs.

If you then total the expenses, and subtract that total from the income, you will have your net profit. Of course, if expenses exceed the income, you will have predicted a net loss. If this is the case, you will need to start reassessing your figures and possibly your business idea to see if it really is feasible.

In any case, your forecast is only a guideline since the success of every new business depends on other variables, such as —

    (a) the capabilities of the owners and employees,

    (b) the location,

    (c) the type of product being sold,

    (d) the market served, and

    (e) the physical facilities.

Sample #1 illustrates an income and expense forecast. Note that not all the headings will be suitable for your business and you may need to add others.

Worksheet #2 is a useful start-up costs worksheet that you can use to estimate your cash needs for the first three months of your enterprise.

BERNARD'S SECONDHAND STORE
Year ending December 31, 199-

INCOME	$110,000
EXPENSES	
Cost of goods sold on consignment	$50,000
Wages and benefits for two employees (including owner at $15,000 per year)	30,000
Depreciation (on equipment costing $5,000)	1,000
Overhead (power, light, heat, and water)	2,000
Equipment repairs	500
Delivery and freight	1,000
Advertising	500
Insurance	300
Rent	12,400
Interest	200
Telephone	800
Taxes	900
Accounting and legal	500
Travel and entertainment	2,000
Miscellaneous	1,200
TOTAL EXPENSES	$103,300
NET PROFIT (Income minus expenses)	$6,700

Worksheet #2
ESTIMATED START-UP COSTS

ITEM	Estimated monthly expenses	Estimated start-up expenses
Owner/manager salary	$ _____ x 2 =	$ _____
Other salaries and wages	_____ x 3 =	_____
Rent	_____ x 3 =	_____
Advertising	_____ x 3 =	_____
Delivery expenses	_____ x 3 =	_____
Supplies	_____ x 3 =	_____
Telephone	_____ x 3 =	_____
Other utilities	_____ x 3 =	_____
Insurance	_____ x 3 =	_____
Taxes	_____ x 3 =	_____
Interest	_____ x 3 =	_____
Maintenance	_____ x 3 =	_____
Legal and professional fees	_____ x 3 =	_____
Other	_____ x 3 =	_____
Fixture and equipment purchase		_____
Decorating and remodeling		_____
Installations of fixtures and equipment		_____
Starting inventory		_____
Licenses and permits		_____
Utilities hook-up charges		_____
Pre-opening advertising and promotion		_____
Cash for unexpected expenses		_____
TOTAL		$ _____

Note: For some businesses, you may have to multiply your estimated monthly expenses by a larger factor than shown here. For example, if you plan to open a seasonal business, you may want a cash reserve to cover six months of operating expenses.

b. Cash flow budget

A cash flow budget measures the flow of money into and out of the business.

There will probably be seasonal fluctuations in your cash flow; in other words, slow months and busy months, times when you'll be cash-poor and times when you'll be cash-rich. You need to be able to predict these times so you can properly finance your business. Your cash flow budget tells you in advance if you'll have enough cash to get by. This budget should be prepared for a one-year period and contain monthly breakdowns. Sample #2 gives an example of a format to use.

If, in plotting out various scenarios using these samples, you discover times when you will have a negative balance going into the next month, you have an early warning that you need to get a loan from somewhere. Especially at the beginning, check your cash flow often to predict when you can expect a crunch.

Computer programs such as Lotus 1-2-3 and Excel are perfect for this kind of forecasting. When you make a change in one place, the program automatically re-adjusts everything in the budget. These programs can be fun, and the time you spend learning them will be a timesaver in the long run.

There are also an increasing number of inexpensive, user-friendly accounting packages, such as Simply Accounting, on the market. These programs can do everything from forecasting, bank reconciliations, and payroll to printing monthly statements and calculating taxes. Many of the features may be more than you think you'll need at first. But as you grow, you'll find yourself needing easy access to many of the more complicated accounting functions. You may decide their ability to grow with you and your business needs make them a more cost-effective alternative than a simple spreadsheet program.

c. Advertising and marketing

Your advertising and marketing budget is one of the biggest variables in your forecasting. Some short-sighted entrepreneurs take the attitude that they will first meet operating expenses and then worry about spending "whatever's left over" on "frills" like advertising.

Sample #2
CASH FLOW BUDGET

	Month				Total
	1	2	3	etc.	
Cash at beginning of month In bank and on hand In investment					
TOTAL CASH					
Income during month Cash sales (include credit cards) Investment income Loans Other cash income					
TOTAL INCOME					
TOTAL CASH AND INCOME					

Expenses during the month
Inventory of new material
Wages and benefits
  (including owner's)
Rent
License and permits
Business taxes
Telephone
Equipment, repairs, and
  rentals
Accounting and legal
Utilities
Advertising
Sales commissions
Delivery and freight
  (including postage)
Vehicle expense
Travel and entertainment
Insurance
Loan repayments
Other cash expenses					

TOTAL EXPENSES					

Cash flow excess (or deficit)
  at end of month
Cash flow cumulative
  (monthly)					

93

With this approach, you will end up with a lot of inventory and a bankrupt business.

d. Murphy's law

You're probably familiar with Murphy's Law — "Anything that can go wrong will go wrong"— or Murphy's First Law of Business — "Everything takes longer than it's supposed to." Starting a business is a lot like doing renovations on a house. No matter how well you plan and budget, somewhere along the line things will go wrong.

With that in mind, add 10% to each individual expense category or actually show a 10% Murphy's Law add-on to the total budget.

e. Cash reserves

Finally, there is the matter of cash reserves. It's obviously desirable to keep some non-working cash in the bank and to have additional funds available for some unanticipated problems or opportunities. There doesn't seem to be a standard rule assessing this amount, but the equivalent of two months of total estimated expenses as the cash reserve amount is a good place to start.

f. Why you need a business plan

As you set up your business you may be asked if you have a business plan. It is not something you need to worry about if you are intent on starting tiny and growing your business out of profits or with a small credit card loan from time to time. The amount of effort that a business plan takes would be much better spent making more sales. However, the day may come when you are ready to move your secondhand business to bigger premises and take a leap that will require you to double or triple your inventory and expenses. When that day comes and you need to get a bank loan or an infusion of cash from investors, you will need to put together a comprehensive business plan.

A business plan is a written document outlining the details of your new business. Preparing your plan will require assistance from your lawyer and your accountant, and considerable research at the public library, trade associations, vendors, and a myriad of other sources. Your plan presents the goals of your business along with a detailed description of the steps necessary to achieve these goals, plus evidence your goals are reasonable and attainable.

It's important to understand that a business plan is not something you just sit down and make up. First of all, such a fantasy document can later come back to haunt you if things go really bad and your lender or investor (quite rightly) alleges fraud. Second, a fantasy document usually won't withstand the questions and scrutiny of even an unsophisticated private investor, let alone a banker or venture capitalist. In putting together this document, you must assemble real evidence that your product or service fills a need and your sales predictions are viable.

Putting together your plan is also a very good imposed discipline which will benefit you in ways other than just helping you get the capital you need. The process of putting together a really good, thorough plan makes you think. It will alert you to opportunities, hazards, and "what if" contingencies you hadn't thought of.

Should you decide to go after major financing, *Preparing a Successful Business Plan*, another book in the Self-Counsel Series, has an example of how to put together a business plan.

g. Sources of funding

Commercial financing holds certain advantages over private funding. Certainly, being able to get all the capital you need from one source, governed by one agreement, as opposed to a patchwork quilt of financing from a collection of private sources, is a big advantage. And you will find it easier to expand and obtain additional financing as needed by having an established borrowing relationship with a commercial lender.

Some sources of funding are —
- Banks
- Finance companies
- Life insurance policies
- Leasing companies
- Vendors
- Home equity credit lines

You may feel less pressure and stress from commercial financing then from having borrowed from friends and relatives.

*A second mortgage
on a home is a
common method of
providing collateral.*

1. Banks

Banks are generally very poor sources of financing for new business ventures, unless you or an associate have substantial personal assets that can be pledged to secure the loan. Bank financing for start-ups will almost always have to be personally or individually secured and collateralized with personal guarantees and property such as stocks, bonds, insurance policies, or real estate.

In truth, this means your "business loan" is a business loan in name only; it's really a personal loan, with you or your other individual guarantor or guarantors placed at maximum risk, unprotected by any corporate shield. What's worse, at the very least there will be lots of questions about your business. You may even have to prepare and submit a business plan — all for what is essentially a personal loan. It is easier to get a loan for buying new furniture than it is to get the same amount for a new small business!

Banks are often better as sources of financing for business re-organization, expansion, or diversification, once a successful track record, sophisticated forecasts, and significant assets are in place.

Even though securing start-up financing from a bank is difficult, it is still the generally preferred source. Many entrepreneurs who are personally guaranteeing or collateralizing loans do deal with banks. And many private backers prefer to put up assets or even cash deposits in banks to secure loans for the business as opposed to making direct loans. And at some point — hopefully in the first few years of business — you'll be able to replace your "patchwork quilt" of start-up financing with a business loan or business financing package from a bank.

(a) Key points

There are several key points to keep in mind whenever approaching a bank for business money.

First, you need to remember that the bank is in the business of lending money, even if it sometimes seems this is not in its game plan. Lending is the bank's primary means of making money for its stockholders. The difference between the interest rate it charges on the loans it makes, less losses and operating costs, and the interest it pays to depositors for the use of their money, is the profit. Although many bankers tell each other that nobody ever got fired for saying no, they know in their hearts this is a half-truth. If they say no too much, profits will dip, and then they *will* get fired. So they are actually looking for good loans to have reasons to say yes.

Second, pay careful attention to the term "good loans." Bankers want to make only good loans. Good loans lead to promotions — bad loans lead to a new job at the car wash. Your job is to convince your banker that the potential of your business constitutes a good loan.

There are, however, many other factors a banker may want to know about that often have nothing to do with your business. For example, if you are personally guaranteeing the loan, your history of honoring obligations and repaying loans is a big issue. If you are providing someone else as a guarantor, that person's history of honoring obligations becomes the issue.

Third, understand that bankers think differently from business people. If you talk to a banker the same way you talk to another entrepreneur, you'll lose every time! Bankers think like bankers. They are not going to get excited about the same things that excite you. They may be incapable of even understanding your business. They will instead focus on the following things because they have been trained to focus on them:

(a) How much money do you need?

(b) How have you come up with that figure? What is the rationale for that figure?

(c) Is it enough?

(d) Is it too much?

(e) How will you make the payments on the loan?

(f) How can the bank be certain you will make your payments?

(g) How is the bank protected in worst case scenarios?

When you have to demonstrate your ability to make the payments, you can draw on a combination of these banker reassurances:

(a) Profit in the business already exceeds the new payments.

(b) You have income from another source that you are willing and able to use if necessary.

(c) You have personal assets which can be liquidated to cover the loan if absolutely necessary.

(b) When the banker says no

Most successful businesspeople have been turned down by a lender at some time in their careers. If your first attempt to raise funds is unsuccessful, don't view it as the end of the line. Turn it into a positive learning experience.

*Don't let the loan
rejection blind you to
the opportunity to
learn and perhaps
improve your
presentation.*

Ask the banker why the loan wasn't approved. Was your business plan lacking some necessary information? Was the problem in your forecast? Was it your market research? The explanation a banker gives you may be just the information you need to ensure you are successful the second, or even the third, fourth, or fifth time. By the time you get to the fifth bank, you'll be ready with some solid answers.

You will find that once a banker has refused a loan, and you've been able to regretfully but graciously accept the fact your request was refused, the pressure is suddenly lifted. Few people will refuse to give advice when asked for it, and a lender is no exception. So don't rush from the bank like a beaten puppy. Stay for a time; a friendly talk could prove worthwhile.

(c) The importance of a good credit rating

Even if he or she is convinced you *can* make the payments, a banker will wonder whether you *will* make the payments, particularly if you encounter difficulties. Obviously your own good credit record and/or that of your guarantor is important here.

If you happen to have had a period of time in your past when some problem — a loss of a job, unexpected bills — caused you to get behind in your bills, but you managed to get caught up and get current again, that story can demonstrate your honorable approach to debt. From a banker's standpoint, a past bankruptcy demonstrates the opposite. If your past will indicate to the banker a willingness on your part to turn your back on obligations, you can definitely count on needing one or more other guarantors with better personal credit histories.

If you are asking that future sales, income, and cash flow be considered as a significant source of funds to meet loan payments, then you're going to need a lot of ammunition to support your forecasts.

If you are pledging tangible collateral, remember that the banker has to evaluate it at liquidation value. A delivery van, for example, might cost you $10,000, but at a bankruptcy auction go for $1,500 or even less! Bankers understand valuing real estate, cars, and negotiable securities. They are much less comfortable with equipment, inventory, and other "business things." You'll have to prove the values you want to attach to such items.

2. Finance companies

As a rule, personal finance companies do not make business loans. However, if you're going to have to personally guarantee the loan you get, and it's a business loan in name only, then there's no really good reason not to borrow in your name, as a personal loan.

Should you use this approach, the goal of replacing the financing with better, true business financing should be paramount in your mind.

3. Life insurance

Many whole-life and universal-life insurance policies build up cash value, which can be withdrawn or borrowed at very low interest rates. Your policy may be in that category.

4. Leasing companies

This is an often overlooked good source of financing. Most business equipment, such as cash registers, fixtures, clothing racks and shelving, and even leasehold improvements and used equipment, can be leased. Leasing companies tend to be more lenient than banks. Unlike bankers, leasing professionals understand business and equipment values, and often know how to re-sell or re-lease repossessed property from deals gone bad. So their worst-case-scenario fears are not nearly as severe as the bankers' might be.

Leasing usually preserves capital. To buy and finance a piece of equipment, you might need to put 30% or more down. Leasing the same equipment might only require first and last month payments.

5. Vendors

You may be able to pay on the installment plan (e.g., half up front and the remainder at a later date) or even arrange a consignment deal (i.e., you don't pay for the item until it is sold) on inventory that you would expect to pay for up front.

6. Home equity credit lines

Use of your home and a second mortgage on your home, or getting another backer to provide funds by placing a second mortgage on his or her home, are two of the most common means of getting money for new business ventures.

In recent years, a different, often more advantageous and flexible form of second mortgage financing has become popular — the "home equity credit line." Banks and finance companies offer credit lines tied to home equity, where you are pre-approved up to a certain amount, issued a checkbook, and set up to write yourself loans against the credit line as needed. This is rapidly becoming the number-one way entrepreneurs are funding the start-up and expansion of their small businesses.

Interest rates on these credit lines typically run at prime plus two or three percentage points, and may be "floating," floating with a cap, or fixed.

Mortgage "closing costs" are usually 1% to 2%, about half that usually charged for other types of mortgages and second mortgages. Sometimes an appraisal, a new title insurance policy, and other miscellaneous costs will be incurred too. To get a backer who will get this kind of credit line in order to turn around and invest in or lend to your business, you'll usually have to agree to reimburse him or her for all these costs.

As a general rule of thumb, a lender will set the credit limit at 75% to 80% of the home's available equity. If a house is appraised at $200,000 and has a balance of $100,000 left on its first mortgage, that leaves $100,000 in available equity at, say, 75%, yielding $75,000 of available credit. However, there are lenders who will make up to 100% of the equity available.

Repayment is often set up with "minimum monthly payments," just like credit cards. Sometimes interest-only minimums are available, with a "balloon payment" or schedule of such principal reduction payments.

Banks, savings-and-loans, credit unions, and personal finance companies and other financial institutions all compete in the home equity credit line business, and offer free booklets and literature about this type of financing.

13

Making your company legal

Once you have decided to open a particular type of secondhand business, and you are sure you have the right qualities to succeed, one of the earliest decisions you have to make is the legal organizational form your enterprise will take.

a. *Proprietorship*

The easiest way for you to establish an organization with little or no cost or legal problems is to operate as a proprietorship. Many retail businesses are operated this way, with the owner responsible for the actions and liabilities of the business, even if the day-to-day running of it, or parts of it, are delegated to others.

The profit of a proprietorship is the personal income of the owner and is taxed, with any salary paid to him or her by the business, at personal tax rates. Any loans from creditors or investors are made to the owner and not to the company.

Proprietorships do not issue shares of any kind as do limited companies (discussed in section c.). Businesses established as proprietorships must still conform to regulatory authorities, such as local licensing authorities, in order to obtain a license to legally operate as a business.

The three common types of organization are the proprietorship, the partnership, and the limited company.

1. Advantages

The main advantages of a proprietorship are that as owner you have total control, do not have to consider the opinions of partners or other business associates (thus speeding the decision-making process), and you will reap the full financial rewards for your efforts.

There are also minimal legal restrictions with a proprietorship and it can be easily discontinued if and when this might be appropriate.

2. Disadvantages

Some disadvantages are that, theoretically, the organization ceases to exist when the owner dies. The assets of the company become part of the owner's estate and are subject to estate and inheritance taxes. Thus it may be difficult for relatives to continue the business.

A proprietorship may also find it difficult to expand since it does not have the same opportunities to raise capital as do other types of business organizations with a broader base of financial resources.

Also, generally speaking, in case of bankruptcy or a serious lawsuit, you may find your personal assets (such as your house, car, and personal savings) as well as the company's assets seized to satisfy the organization's liabilities. In other words, the proprietorship's liability is unlimited. This is the major disadvantage of a proprietorship.

b. Partnership

Unlike the sole proprietorship, a partnership is generally a more formal type of business organization. It is a legal association between two or more individuals as co-owners of a business.

Although a partnership does not require a written agreement, all partners should agree to a negotiated contract, or articles of partnership. The terms of these articles vary widely from one enterprise to another, but they should include at least the name of the company; the name of each partner; the rights, contributions, and benefits of each partner; how the profits and losses are to be distributed (without an agreement to the contrary they are assumed to be distributed equally); and the length of the life of the partnership.

In a partnership, each partner may represent the company and enter into contracts on its behalf. Each partner is also personally liable for the debts of the company incurred by other partners. This personal liability (as with a proprietorship) is unlimited.

Partnerships are not taxed at the limited company tax rates. Instead, the business's net income, or loss, is shared according to the terms of the partnership contract, and each partner includes that share, plus any salary received from the company, on his or her personal tax return.

Partnerships, like proprietorships, do not issue shares of any kind and must conform to regulatory authorities.

1. Advantages

The main advantages of partnerships are that they are relatively easy to organize, financing is sometimes easier to obtain, and (since there is more than one owner) the total partnership investment can be much greater than in a proprietorship. A partnership may also have a greater depth of combined judgment and managerial skills.

2. Disadvantages

Disadvantages are that, except in the case of limited partnerships (discussed later), upon one partner's death or withdrawal from the business, the partnership may have to be dissolved and reorganized. This can make it difficult to continue the company's operations.

It can also create financial difficulties for the business if the dead partner's heirs disagree with the company's evaluation of his or her share of the company. Also, the heirs have to be bought out, which may impose a financial burden on the remaining partners.

Another disadvantage of the partnership is that, since in many cases all partners need to be consulted, quick decisions about the company's operations may be difficult to make and serious disagreements can occur.

Also, partners are not only responsible for the debts and obligations they have contracted for, but they are also responsible for those contracted by all other partners. You could find yourself legally required to pay for that yacht one of the partners bought for the business.

Finally, it may be difficult to remove an incompetent partner or one you don't get along with. Difficulties often arise with partners concerning the direction the business should take and how it should be run. Sometimes considerable interpersonal skills are necessary to overcome these difficulties. This is the most serious drawback of a partnership arrangement. More partnerships have foundered on differences between partners than any other reason.

However, these difficulties in themselves can also be opportunities since, in discussing them, mutually agreeable objectives and plans often materialize. This can be an advantage compared to operating as a proprietorship where you may have no one knowledgeable about your business to discuss it with.

To minimize areas of conflict in a partnership you might consider including in the partnership agreement details concerning the following typical questions:

(a) Who is responsible for various aspects of the business, for example, production and marketing?

(b) Who establishes operating policies and, indeed, what constitutes a policy? Are policies, or changes of policies, decided by a majority vote of the partners, or by some other method?

(c) What expenses (for example, car mileage or entertainment expenses) can be charged to the business?

c. *Limited company*

Many small businesses are organized as limited companies. The limited company, unlike the proprietorship and partnership, is a separate legal entity, with its own rights and duties, and can continue as a separate organization even after the death of an owner.

A limited company can be created for any size of business; it is wrong to consider it appropriate only for larger companies.

Establishing a limited company is both more complex and more costly (from a legal and accounting point of view) than establishing a proprietorship or a partnership but, despite these problems, is an effective way of operating a business.

For regulatory purposes, a limited company is like a person. It can sue and be sued, just like an individual, and it must conform to regulatory authorities. A limited company is an ongoing organization with an infinite life of its own even though employees and owners come and go. Many of its assets, such as land and buildings, may indeed have a longer life than the life of the shareholders.

1. *Public versus private companies*

Limited companies may be established as either public or private. A public company is generally one that has its shares listed on a stock exchange. The legal requirements for operating a public company are much more strict than those for a private company. However, you will more likely be interested in organizing a private limited company since that type of company is designed for the small business operator.

A private company is one that is:

(a) restricted in its right to transfer shares,

(b) limited to a maximum number of shareholders, and

(c) prohibited from offering its shares to the public.

The regulations governing private corporations change from time to time. Consult your lawyer about the current requirements when you want to incorporate.

2. Incorporation

Companies can be incorporated in a single state or province, in one or more states or provinces, or federally. Since you will probably start out by operating your business in a single location, you need to incorporate only in that jurisdiction and then register in other jurisdictions as required.

You can have a lawyer set up the limited company for you or, in many cases, you can do this for yourself since books are available that show you, step by step, how this is done.

Doing it yourself may save you several hundred dollars. However, if the situation is complex, professional legal advice should be sought. For example, depending on your personal financial situation, there may be advantages to establishing the share structure of the company one way rather than another.

3. Advantages of incorporating

The major advantage of the limited company form of business is that, generally speaking, since the company is a separate legal entity, the individual owners cannot be held responsible for the company's liabilities. The owners, in other words, have a liability limited to their investment in shares in the company.

However, despite this, lending institutions you approach for financing usually make you sign a personal note to extend your liability outside the protection offered by the company. This is particularly true for a new business.

Another advantage is that financing may be facilitated by the creation of easily transferable certificates of ownership, known as shares, which may be bought by or sold to others, including employees of the company.

This broadens the base of financing available to the company. The limited liability of share ownership appeals to some investors since it permits ownership, with a potential return on the investment, without involvement in the company's day-to-day operations.

There may also be some personal tax advantages to forming a limited company that make this form of business appealing.

4. Disadvantages of incorporating

Some disadvantages of the limited company include: decision making — depending on the company's size and number of owners, decision making can be a lengthy process; and dilution of control and profits can also occur if there are a great many shareholders (although this would not normally be true of the typical private limited company).

Also, double taxation exists for shareholders of limited companies. The corporation pays taxes on its profit at the corporate tax rate. Any after-tax income may be distributed to the individual shareholders as dividends. The individual is then taxed on these dividends at personal tax rates.

A limited company is also subject to more government regulation and form remittance than a proprietorship or a partnership, although this is a small price to pay considering the advantages incorporation may offer.

d. S corporations (U.S. only)

Federal income taxes have an important and decided impact on the legal form of organization. Sometimes it is preferable for a proprietorship or partnership to become incorporated, at other times it is not. Since this can be a very complex subject, individual situations must be investigated on their own merits and the advice of a tax accountant considered.

In the U.S., however, you do have a tax option known as an S corporation. The philosophy behind the S corporation provisions of the internal revenue code is that a business should be able to choose its organizational form free of tax considerations. In essence, this type of corporation allows the business to operate with the highly advantageous limited liability for its owners, but without the

Each situation is different. Consult your accountant for the tax pros and cons of forming a limited company to suit your particular situation.

corporate penalty of double taxation mentioned earlier, since an S corporation pays tax like a partnership.

To qualify, a corporation must —

(a) have no more than 35 stockholders,

(b) be a domestic corporation, and

(c) have only one class of stock.

These qualifications change from time to time and it would be wise to discuss the S corporation form of business with your tax adviser before making any decision.

e. *Legal form and sale of business*

Finally, give some thought, even when starting out, to eventual sale or disposition of your business. This is something you should discuss with your accountant and lawyer since it can affect the legal form of business you initially set up, the income taxes you may have to pay when you retire and sell your business, or when the business passes to your heirs upon your death.

f. *What's in a name?*

Just like a baby, a company must have a name. However, it's sometimes harder to choose a company name than to choose a name for a baby. When you decide on your company name, you must pick one that is acceptable to:

(a) the Secretary of State in the United States, or

(b) the provincial Registrar in Canada.

A name will usually be approved as long as it is not identical to or does not closely resemble any existing company names. Names that are similar to existing company names may cause confusion and are generally not allowed.

Try to choose a name that is both distinctive and describes your type of business. A name like "Re-Runs and Collectibles, Ltd." would be a better name for your secondhand business than "Western Enterprises, Ltd." The word *Western* has been used so often that it is no longer distinctive. Other words which fall into the no-longer-distinctive category are *Northern, American,* and *Universal.*

Enterprises as the second element of the name also does not accurately describe the nature of a secondhand store. It might be more appropriate in connection with an investment company.

Try to stay away from words such as *Institute, Condominium,* or *Co-operative,* which in many states and provinces are restricted to specific organizations.

A coined or made-up word, perhaps a combination of your name and your partner's, plus a descriptive word (e.g., Jenbar Collectibles, Ltd.) is usually a safe choice for a company name.

If you decide to use your own full name as the company name, remember the drawbacks. People may use your company name to find your home phone number and phone you there at inconvenient hours. In the event of bankruptcy, your name shares the stigma of the failed company. When you sell the business, your name goes with it, and should the business fall into bankruptcy, the damage to your name will be the same as if you had gone bankrupt yourself.

If you use a street or location in your company name, you may run into problems if you move. For example, Carnaby Street Collectibles is great where your store is located on Carnaby Street, but less so when your rent increases dramatically and you decide to move 15 blocks away.

In Canada, many registrars have to routinely refuse names that imply a connection with or the approval of the royal family. For this reason, names using words such as *Imperial* or *Royal* will be rejected, as well as names implying the approval of a branch, service, or department of the government.

A name that could be construed as obscene, or is too general in that it describes only the quality, goods, or function of the services, will be rejected. Already existing companies, such as *General Motors* and *Best Foods,* have more or less monopolized these choices.

Avoid names and well-known abbreviations of companies already in existence. A name like *Xerox Construction Co.* implies a connection with Xerox. Xerox may sue you for trying to pass off their company name as your own.

Whatever name you chose, if you incorporate, your name must end with *Limited, Incorporated,* or *Corporation,* or the abbreviation of one of these words.

You can check for existing company names in your telephone directory and trade and corporation directories at your local library.

14

Pay up: licenses and permits

Welcome to the bureaucracy. Trekking from one office to another, filling out forms, and paying fees is not anyone's idea of fun, but failing to have one necessary permit can cause you a lot more grief and expense later.

a. *United States*

The following list includes the licenses and permits you may have to obtain. Depending on your location and the nature of your business, some of these will not apply to you.

1. *Business licenses and/or sales tax licenses*

As a business owner, you have the privilege of collecting taxes from your customers on behalf of the government, accounting for these taxes, and passing them along to the government — as a free service! So, for each "taxing district," such as the state or states you operate in, the county or counties, and the city or cities, you'll need sales tax licenses. Your accountant should be able to advise you on the licenses you need and the specific taxes you need to collect and pay.

Always check with your local authorities as to which licenses and permits you will need.

2. Fire department permit

If you will be using or storing flammable chemicals, you must obtain this permit. All buildings regardless of use may be subject to a fire department inspection.

3. Sign permits

Most districts have ordinances governing the types and sizes of signs you can place on the exterior of buildings, on sign posts, and on your vehicles, and there can be sizable fines for violating these ordinances.

The best way to deal with the agencies that administer these licenses and taxes and to get all the permits you need is to first call them and ask about their requirements, their office hours, whether or not they accept checks, and so on. Some may be willing to send you the forms by mail. With this kind of advance planning, you can get organized to make the rounds and file all the forms in one day.

b. Canada

1. Goods and services tax (GST)

The 7% GST is charged on almost all goods and services in Canada. You will have to charge GST on goods and services you provide and pay it on purchases you make.

If you expect your gross revenue to be over $30,000, you must register with Revenue Canada in order to:

(a) charge and collect the tax, and

(b) recover the GST you have been charged on items for your business.

If you expect your gross revenue to be under $30,000, you need not register or collect GST. However, if you do not register, you will not be able to recover GST you pay for business purchases.

If you are doing business in Nova Scotia, New Brunswick, or Newfoundland, you will be required to collect and remit the 15% Harmonized Sales Tax (HST) which replaces the current retail sales taxes and the GST in those provinces.

For more information on GST and HST, call the government's local taxation office.

2. Provincial sales tax

Every province except Alberta imposes a sales or social service tax on goods sold in the province. As with the GST, you can register for provincial sales tax and be exempt from paying tax on merchandise purchased for resale or tax on merchandise that will become a part of tangible personal property intended for resale.

3. Municipal laws and regulations

(a) Licensing

All municipalities may issue licenses and permits based on local bylaws. Municipalities also control aspects of —

- (a) zoning,
- (b) land use,
- (c) construction,
- (d) renovation, and
- (e) licensing for commercial vehicles.

(b) Taxes

Municipalities may tax —

- (a) real estate,
- (b) water consumption, and
- (c) business practices.

(c) Building requirements

While all levels of government have some responsibility for regulating commercial building, municipal governments bring together all the various building codes and inspections, making it possible for you to get approval at the local level.

(d) Hospitalization

Some provinces require that regular amounts be paid into a province-wide hospital plan. The payments can be made by employees directly or as a payroll deduction by employees and employer together.

c. Zoning laws

Cities usually zone different areas according to intended use. There will be areas zoned for residential only, some for retail and "light commercial" businesses only, and some areas for anything including "heavy industrial." There will also be certain zoning laws governing very specific types of businesses, such as the number of miles required between a tavern and a church or the amount of off-street parking required for a certain type of business.

If you are renting or leasing commercial space or buying a commercial building, you will want to be certain these zoning laws permit the operation of your planned business on those premises. If you are using the services of a real estate or leasing agent, that person should be able to provide you with information or documentation from the zoning and commercial inspection people in your city's government regarding the legality of your business at the location in question.

If you have to trek down to your local city hall yourself to find this out, brace yourself for a day of bureaucratic agony, smile and be courteous, but be persistent until you get your questions answered.

Zoning laws are of particular concern to people operating home-based businesses. The fastest growing part of the entrepreneurial world is the home-based business, and most zoning laws are antiquated in their handling of this. Over half of all home-based businesses may be illegal according to the governing zoning laws. When you look into zoning in your area, you may find there are restrictions on odor, noise, excess traffic, pollution, and other problems businesses may cause. You may also find other rules that severely limit your ability to operate, such as not being allowed to sell retail or employ anyone other than family members.

Many local governments already make allowances for secondary use of the home for business. Others are so restrictive they prohibit home-based businesses completely. Fortunately, such areas are the exception, but if you do find yourself living in such an area, you can apply for a zoning variance that will allow your business to operate. You may not get it, but you can at least try.

If you're going to operate a home-based business, the bottom line is to avoid inconveniencing or annoying your neighbors. Even if you have a perfect right to operate a business there, you don't want to poison your dealings with your neighbors by making a lot of noise, dust, or traffic.

Your business neighbors can also be helpful in filling you in about prevailing laws and the proper government agencies to contact.

15
Insurance

a. *Loss of or damage to property*

You can, and should, insure to cover loss of or damage to property. This kind of insurance is considered basic for most businesses. Many leases require your business have it. However, as a practical matter, many businesses "go naked" and risk operating without this expense, at least in the start-up months.

Insured or not, you should do everything you can to prevent the catastrophic loss of your assets. Your computer files should be regularly backed up with safe copies stored away from your business premises. Your business premises should have burglar alarms and window decals, fire alarms, and fire extinguishers. You don't need to be an electronics genius to take on all this as a do-it-yourself project with supplies from a security supply company in your area.

You also need to protect yourself against claims for damage to customer's property and your store property, whether they are to fixed assets, equipment, or to the building itself. As soon as an incident occurs, note the details, such as the date and time of the accident, the weather conditions, if relevant, and details of the accident. Also record your response or your employee's response to the accident, as well as the names of all people involved, including employees, customers, and witnesses.

You can and probably should buy business interruption insurance that provides protection for loss of income due to disruption of business.

b. Injuries to employees or customers

Injuries to employees or customers should also be insured against. Beyond that, you have a responsibility to be sure your open-to-the-public and work environments are as safe as possible. Crowded, badly lit isles can be a hazard. A customer who trips or has a heavy object fall on him or her from overhead could put you out of business or worse unless you take special care and are insured.

Again, *Cut Your Losses,* another book in the Self-Counsel Series, discusses personal injury claims in more detail, including fraud artists.

Again, it is important to record any accident as soon as it occurs. Even minor accidents can turn into major lawsuits. Record details such as the date, time, location, and names and addresses of those involved, including that of any witnesses to the accident. Also make a note of whether any medical attention was given. Check with your insurance agent or local authorities about first aid requirements you should be aware of as a retailer.

Also check with your local authorities whether there is a specific form you need to use to report employee injuries.

Making sure your store is safe is your best insurance against accidents.

c. Disability or death of a key person in the business

Disability or death of a key person in the business, too, can be insured against. And in many true entrepreneurial situations there really is no other solution to this risk. If you have family to be concerned about, you should at least have term life insurance on yourself along with a buy-sell agreement (see your lawyer). Here are some other arrangements you need to make in case you or your partner(s) should die —

(a) prepare a will, and

(b) keep a list of important information including locations of keys and vital documents.

d. Counterfeiting, forgery, and robbery

Though not common, counterfeiting, forgery, and robbery can create big losses. Your insurance broker can make sure you are covered for these perils and your local police can help you with counterfeiting identification and robbery procedures. Here are a few useful suggestions:

- NEVER try to stop a robbery. Your personal safety and those of your employees and customers are your only responsibility. Your insurance will cover your loss.

- The biggest source of forgery in the secondhand business is the simple note that gives permission to the bearer to sell the goods in his or her possession to you. The second source of forgeries is bad checks. Both can usually be prevented by using common sense and sticking to the policies designed to stop bad checks.

e. Vehicle accidents

Even before you own a store, you will probably have a delivery vehicle for buying and delivering goods. Again, check with your local authorities or insurance agent about insurance requirements for either a company vehicle or personal vehicle used for business. In some places you can use your own car for business without increasing the premiums, while in many cases, special insurance rates apply. Failure to have the correct insurance can create big problems.

Part IV
Minding the store

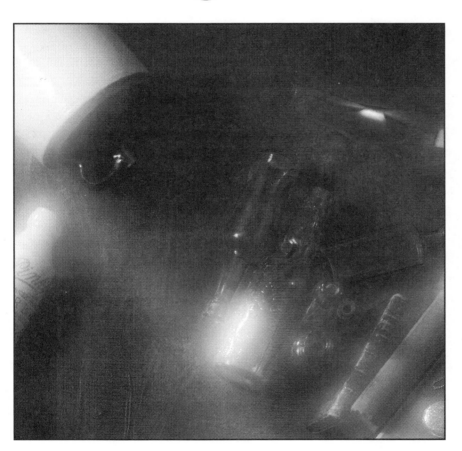

16

What's it going to look like?

Your store layout is a critical factor in merchandising your products. It is never too early to think about the layout of your store and training your sales employees with the objective of maximizing sales.

Although you will be primarily concerned with the internal layout of your retail store, the external appearance of your shop can have an important bearing on whether customers are attracted inside.

a. *External appearance*

Potential customers judge your store on their initial reaction to its external appearance. External appearance includes the state of repair and cleanliness (e.g., paint or other exterior wall covering), as well as the cleanliness of your sidewalk. The sidewalk should be kept clear of dust, dirt, trash, snow, and slush at all times.

1. *Signs*

External signs should be kept in good condition. A sign should communicate simply and briefly the type of business you are in and the type of products or services you offer. Keep in mind whether it is to be read by passing motorists or pedestrians, or both. If your sign has to be read at night, make sure the lighting is adequate.

Some merchandisers advocate keeping displays free of clutter while others think a cornucopia of unique secondhand goods is a feast for passersby. Whatever you choose, make it attractive.

An angled or canted window display is more interesting than a flat left to right scene.

Before contracting for or erecting any external sign, check that there are no limitations imposed by the city or your rental contract. It is expensive to have a sign produced that you cannot use because it is larger than allowed.

2. Window display

The external appearance of your shop also includes what the customer can see of the inside of your store from outside, such as the window display.

This display should be kept current (i.e., regular display rotation as frequently as every two weeks), with fresh prices or other eye-catching signs that are professionally prepared, not felt-penned onto old squares of cardboard. You can do wonders with a computer, so even if you are not artistic, there is little excuse for messy signage.

Consider your window as a stage when planning displays. In other words, the center foreground is the location of your prime display items, the sides and rear for secondary displays.

Take advantage of themes, seasons, holidays, and other events to make your display interesting and appealing. An interesting display can attract window shoppers into your store and turn them into purchasers.

If display lights are used, plan where you place those lights carefully to minimize window glare. Do not have spotlights shining outward to dazzle window shoppers.

Keep your windows clean. Dirty windows can be detrimental to attracting customers. As much as possible keep your window clear of signs. Glass is made to see through, although there are occasions when "sale" signs are needed to attract the customers' attention.

Remember, a window display is part of your business's promotion. The attractiveness of your store's exterior, including the window display, is especially important if you are opening in premises which are new or in an outlet that previously provided different products and/or services. The exterior must tell potential customers that you are new and you have something special to offer them.

3. The front sidewalk

Most cities have bylaws governing what you can put on the front sidewalk. In our city, for example, sandwich boards are restricted and the sidewalk is supposed to be clear. However, the rules are rarely enforced, so colorful displays of goods frequently crowd the walk closest to the door of secondhand stores. Clothes flap in the

Theft from outdoor displays is always a potential problem, so any goods you display should be ones that take two strong men to move, are of little value, or are roped down.

breeze on hooks on the exterior of buildings and merchants generally take advantage of every conceivable cranny to display their wares. Nothing advertises your wares like a cluttered front street.

If the rules in your area are strictly enforced, you might try getting a variance that will allow you to fence off a small area similar to the areas outside many outdoor cafes. Don't go overboard. Remember, one downside of having a huge outdoor space filled with goods is that you have to haul them in when you close or anytime it rains.

Remember, though, that you have a responsibility to be sure your open-to-the-public and work environments are as safe as possible. Especially in a general secondhand store, crowded badly lit aisles can be a hazard, and corded sidewalks or low hanging signs can cause injures that could result in lawsuits. Be sure to have liability insurance available along with your fire and theft insurance. Chapter 15 discusses insurance needs in further detail.

b. Interior

The exterior of your store may help attract some customers, but it is the interior decor and atmosphere, combined with the assistance and attitude of salespeople, that can convert potential customers into purchasers. The interior of your store, like the exterior, must be compatible with your products and the image you are trying to portray.

1. Layout

Layout is probably one of the most critical factors in all retail merchandising. The objective in retailing is to sell, and the way a store is laid out can be an extremely effective tool in maximizing sales.

The layout of any store depends on the amount of space available and the type of products. For example, a general secondhand goods or computer store will have a completely different type of display and layout from a clothing store since the clothing store has to allow space for fitting rooms. However, in all cases, the objective is to effectively display merchandise.

In very small stores, layout is inflexible. A counter where one or more employees work separates customers from the entire merchandise display that is behind the counter. This is especially common in shared space arrangements.

The more temptations customers pass, the greater the chance they will buy something. Group your best wares near the front door to zap the customers as they come in.

Although secondhand stores are notoriously overcrowded, try to create an air of spaciousness in displays, and wherever possible, avoid displays that block the view of other parts of the store or location of cashiers.

In larger stores, there may be more display areas around the remaining walls. In even larger stores, there may be counters or rack displays around which customers must circulate to select items.

2. Use of space

Use space effectively. Know the value of your space and locate merchandise accordingly.

Prime merchandise (for example, items with the highest profit margins) should be near the front of the store since that space is the most valuable. It is here in the highest traffic area that impulse merchandise and convenience goods should be located.

Cash register stands are also good locations for impulse items. Place sale merchandise or other special items in a wide aisle and use a special display rack for effective merchandising. Customers will become used to looking for specials in that particular location.

Specialists in store layout say the front third of a store should provide 50% of total sales, and the back two-thirds the remaining 50%.

3. Non-selling activities

You should separate selling from non-selling activities. In other words, keep accounting and areas for similar functions separate from the main area of the store — where you are selling merchandise. Generally, these non-sales functions should be at the back of the shop since the front of any store is prime merchandising space.

Research has shown that no one likes to take the first slice of pie. The same can be said for perfectly stacked goods. Take an item or so out of your display to make it more inviting.

4. Aisles

There are basically two types of retail store customer: those who know what they want when they come into the store and actively look for it or ask for it immediately, and those who are just browsers without specific buying objectives but who might buy something if it appeals to them. You want your store layout to entice them both.

Main aisles should be set up from the main door(s) since that is where customer traffic will be the heaviest as people enter and exit. Counters on either side of a main aisle are generally more effective than subsidiary aisles in catching your customers' attention. Subsidiary aisles, if there are any, should be off to the sides. Customers frequently stop for an extended period of time to look at the first goods they see as they enter.

Counters at either end of aisles are also good spots for catching attention and are good locations for special displays, sale items, new items, loss leaders, and similar goods.

All aisles should be as wide as is practical to minimize crowding and better display the merchandise. Remember, too, that you may be moving furniture or other large items through this space each day. It is always a shock when you have to spend 30 minutes rearranging your aisles to remove a trunk you put in the middle of the store a month ago.

5. Fixtures and equipment

Use display fixtures and equipment that compliment the decor of your interior. If you are displaying antique watches, use an old case, not a shiny chrome and glass job. However, if you have only a limited budget for fixtures, you may be wiser to purchase or rent less expensive fixtures rather than cut back on the amount of inventory on display. It is selling inventory (not the quality of your display fixtures and equipment) that provides you with profit and cash flow.

6. Displays

Do not overcrowd displays. Too crowded a display can confuse customers and may prevent them from easily spotting something they are looking for or would buy if it were more obviously visible. A choice between two or three similar products is easier and more likely than if five or six are on display.

Group displays into obvious categories and do not constantly move products to different locations, since that can irritate repeat customers.

The objective of good display is to make the items most customers want stand out. Display signs, where appropriate, can help, but don't overdo them since a clutter of signs can detract from the actual merchandise displays. Poor signs detract, so however many you use, have them professionally done.

If you advertise that you have a sale on certain items, special sale signs should highlight the location of those items.

The color of signs are important for visual impact. Sale signs are often red letters with a yellow background. But black or red letters on white also stand out well.

7. Environment

Make good use of light, ventilation, and heat for customer and employee comfort. Without pleasant surroundings, customers can be discouraged and unhappy employees can add further discouragement.

Use colors on walls, ceiling, and floor coverings with discretion. Bold colors can appear aggressive and inappropriate except in special situations. Colors that blend in well are preferable in most cases since they should serve primarily as a backdrop to your merchandise displays and should not overwhelm them.

However, some bright colors (such as orange, yellow, or even white) in moderate amounts can be helpful in highlighting some of your lower priced merchandise.

17
Inventory control

Keeping track of inventory is one of those chores everyone loves to hate. The somewhat romanticized image that most frequently comes to mind is one of long hours perched atop a stool laboring over thick ledger books while attempting (usually without much success) to keep the Dickensian cold from permeating your bones.

Relax. Take your scarf off. Things have changed dramatically and much for the better since the days of Scrooge and Marley. Here are some tips that will work for you, not against you, on the fast track to inventory control.

a. Consignment

Building your stock by taking goods on consignment is both an expected standard and a smart business practice for most second-hand dealers. Because you don't have to pay for goods outright, you'll be able to build a sizable inventory without needing cash up front — a real bonus for any business, whether new or established. Be sure to indicate that you accept goods on consignment in any advertising you do and on a sign near the cash register.

Once you've established a reputation, you'll often find you have more stock than you can comfortably handle, and you'll be able to choose only what you think will be the fastest moving product. Part I discusses consignment of particular product — books, clothing, computers, and sporting goods — in more detail. Sample #3 shows a typical consignment agreement.

b. *The numbers don't lie*

No matter how you plan to keep track of your inventory, the first step is always the same: assign each item a number as soon as it comes through the front door. "We number absolutely everything," says one household goods dealer. "Even if it's just a salt and pepper shaker we bought ourselves at a garage sale, it gets a number. That way I can always keep on top of where things come from, and I know what our best sources of income are."

The purpose of any numbering system is to allow you to keep track of your inventory more easily. If you have a particular method of numbering that you like and are comfortable with, use it.

The most straightforward method is to make these numbers sequential, although many dealers also like to include a letter code to help identify the owner, especially if the goods are brought in on consignment. For example, the set of silver teaspoons brought in by May Barnett might be coded *1156 MB*.

Some people prefer to make the identity number do triple duty and use it to show when the item was bought in. A code of 97-03-1156-MB would indicate May Barnett's spoons were brought into the store during March of 1997. This method works well if you are willing to hang on to items for a long period of time without discounting them. Many collectible and antique dealers use this method.

c. *So just what is item #45JN-6658-96B?*

Along with the inventory control number, you'll need to keep track of exactly what it is — a spoon set, a baseball bat, a first edition, or a silver charm bracelet? If it's a common item, you should also include any pertinent details to help you distinguish it from the rest of your stock. As one sporting goods manager pointed out, "When you're looking at a shelf with 50 bicycle helmets, it sure helps to know which brand and color you're looking for." The amount of detail you include will vary, but here are some hints to get you going:

- Color: if you have six sofas on the floor, it's helpful to know if you're looking for the white one or the blue floral.

- Size isn't just for clothing. Bicycles come in different sized frames and a chest of drawers can have two, three, six, or more drawers.

126

- Other details may be included if appropriate:
    (a) Serial number
    (b) Brand name
    (c) Model
    (d) Year of manufacture
- Distinguishing marks and/or flaws not only help you find the item on the shelf, but if a customer tries to return a brass vase because "it's got a dent in it," you can immediately prove the dent was already there when that customer bought it. See Sample #4 for a basic manual inventory control form. Chapter 18 discusses "as is" policies.

d. Show your price

Once you have assigned an identity number, tag the item showing both the price and the tracking number. Many experienced dealers also use some kind of color coding to help them easily identify items on the shelf which are due for discount. It's much faster to scan your stock for items tagged with green and mark them down on the spot than it is to follow up from the master list to the shelf.

Color coding also simplifies the store-wide discounts which can be an effective method of inventory reduction. For example, "All skirts with green tags are 20% off today only" makes a great attention grabber as a sign on the street and requires no outlay of time for you to go through the store marking everything down.

See chapter 18 for a discussion of setting prices.

e. Store credits

When accepting product from sellers, most secondhand stores, especially secondhand bookstores, offer sellers a choice between cash payment outright or credit against in-store purchases. Cash purchases allow you to pay the seller less (usually about half of what you would give for a store credit), and once you have made the purchase, you simply put the product on the shelves — no follow up needed. The disadvantage to cash purchases is that they are a drain on your cash flow.

Store credits, on the other hand, let you keep your working cash available but mean you will make less on future sales because a

Items such as television sets that are missing their serial number or have the serial number obscured in any way should not be accepted, as they are most likely stolen property. Report anyone attempting to sell this type of product to the police immediately.

Sample #3
INVENTORY LIST

Inventory item #	Date purchased	Description	Wholesale price	Date sold	Retail price
MB 104	23/02	teaspoons (5)	5.00	04/03	9.95
GL 309	23/02	wooden platter	2.00	21/03	4.95
GL 310	"	salad bowl (chipped edge)	4.00		
ST 498	02/03	Eygptian vase	10.00	09/05	15.95
ST 499		bell	auction		
ST 500		copper pot		01/04	2.50

Reproduced courtesy of Dorothy Volchof

portion of the selling price will be in store credit. However, since you know these customers will be back to claim their credits, you are also guaranteeing an ongoing customer base.

Here are some tips when dealing with store credits.

(a) Keeping track of credits as they go through the cycle of being used up and increased again can be as simple as recording the customer's name on an index card and keeping a running balance. Database programs look fancy, but they are also cumbersome and time consuming unless you are tracking each item individually or you really love computers.

(b) Allow only a portion of purchases to be made with store credit so you always have some cash coming in from every sale. Percentages vary: 50% is the most common amount, although you might want to consider 75% if you have a steady turnover. Remember, though, that if you carry any new product, you can't afford the luxury of allowing store credit to be used toward its purchase. Even with a 100% mark up, a new item that sells for $10 will cost you $5. If you allow 50% store credit, you'll only cover your costs. And if you allow a 75% credit, the sale actually costs you $2.50!

(c) Consider giving an automatic 50% store credit of the price paid if the item is returned within 60 days. This technique is used effectively by a small number of stores to encourage repeat business.

Rule of thumb: a store credit is worth approximately double the cash purchase price. So you would pay $1 cash or give a $2 store credit.

f. I've had this fish tank long enough

There comes a point when product has taken up space in your store for long enough. Perhaps you have no room for the truck load of treasures from last week's estate sale or auction, perhaps you want to revamp your displays, perhaps the fish tank has just been sitting on the shelf for too many months without sparking a single splash of interest. Eventually, you will need to get rid of certain items. Here are some ideas to help you free up space.

1. Put it on sale

One of the main reasons people shop in secondhand stores is because they're looking for bargains. So the better the bargains, the greater your chances of moving out the goods.

If the items are small, many dealers create a "Super Savings" bin at the front of the store. This can be a table of "Discount books: $1

No matter what you sell, poorly done patch jobs drop the value. If you can't do a quality repair, leave it as it is.

per foot" (be sure to have a ruler hanging on the wall so people can measure out their great bargains) or grab bags of miscellaneous odds and ends that the customer purchases for the thrill of finding out just what is inside. Perhaps you want to put all ceramic flower pots at 50% off the last ticketed price or hang a big sign by the cash register so everyone will know that all items with a blue dot are two for one.

Deep discounts like this are usually a last attempt to move product. If the item still doesn't sell, you will have to consider some more drastic measures.

2. *Repair and retry*

Certain items such as furniture may sell better with a face-lift. Try a new coat of paint or a fresh stain after sanding out the scuff marks. Filling cracks in ceramics or replacing broken leaded glass panels can sometimes make all the difference in a customer's mind, plus you will usually be able to charge more!

Warning: If you are dealing in antiques or collectibles, repairs may lower the price you can charge. Be sure you research this before you begin.

3. *Donate it to charity*

It's tough to give away something you've paid good money for, but sometimes, this is the best answer. In any city there are numerous organizations constantly looking for clothing, household goods, and even toys for families in need. If you can't sell it, and you need the space for product that will sell, giving to charity helps solve your problem and someone else's as well.

4. *For procrastinators only — rearrange your displays*

To clean furniture, Ho-Jo, a mechanic's hand cleaner works great on even Victorian or Georgian antiques.

If you just can't bring yourself to get rid of an item, a last resort is to rearrange your store. Usually this is simply a lot of work for very little gain. Often, it aggravates the problem, as things get piled higher and deeper until soon not only can you not see what you have but neither can your customers.

g. *Dutch auction — keeping your stock rotating*

Dutch auction only in Holland? Hardly. Dutch auction is the most common method used to keep product moving, especially in a consignment store. The principle is simple: the price of an item drops by a certain percentage over time, for example, 10% every two weeks. While it's important to get input from the consignors so you know what their expectations are, you as store owner should set the starting sale price of the items in all but rare circumstances. Be prepared to turn down an occasional item if the consignor insists on a price that you believe is unrealistically high.

Here's how Dutch auction affects the price of a $50 evening gown:

Selling price during week 1 = $50

Selling price during week 3 = $45

Selling price during week 5 = $40

Following this progression, by the middle of the third month, the price on the dress will have dropped to half of its original amount. Some secondhand stores allow the price to continue falling until it reaches zero. At that point, the store owns the item. Others prefer to stop when an item plunges to 50% or after a certain length of time, for example, six months. Often this decision is based on the amount of space available. "Customers don't want to keep seeing the same old stuff in a store," says one general goods dealer who uses this method to ensure a steady turnover in her stock.

If you are short on space in your store, consider how long you can allow an item to take up space if it isn't selling.

h. So where and how do I record all this detail?

1. The traditional method

Traditionally, records have been kept in three-ring binders, notebooks, or on index cards stored in anything from a shoebox to a defunct fish tank. Time and thousands of successful secondhand dealers have proved you do not need anything fancier than this. Sure it's nice to have a fancy, leather-bound ledger book and a gold pen to make your daily entries with. But these frills aren't *necessary*. Ultimately, the only questions you must answer are:

- Is it easy for me to handle? Keep in mind that very small books can be awkward physically to pick up, write in, and read.

- Is it easy for me to keep within reach so I can record things whenever I have a few moments? Record books and storage containers should be durable and portable.

- Is the entry format simple enough that can I keep it updated with a minimum of time and effort? If it takes you half an hour just to get your bookkeeping system set up for entry or you must enter each transaction in four different places, you need to consider a more basic version.

- Can I cross-reference the item number with sales? As long as you mark the correct item number on the sales slip, you will always be able to go back to the original record of incoming product.

2. *The new wave — computerized inventory control*

Computers have opened up a whole new world of single-entry inventory control systems. Database programs simplify the process of recording, tracking, discounting, and billing, plus make it easy for you to produce an infinite variety of business reports and projections with just a few keystrokes. There's often no need to go to your accountant except at year end.

If you are running a consignment store, you already know it's essential to track each and every purchase from the time you receive it until you pay the owner. Here's where a computerized tracking system really shines.

"Consignment stores have many unique needs when it comes to tracking inventory," explains Ken Wharton, founder of Black Tie Systems Group Inc. "Since the store doesn't own consignment inventory, it doesn't become part of the company assets and can't have a cost of goods assigned to it. But most secondhand stores sell some new products as well, and this stock is an asset and must be recorded as such."

To further complicate the tracking process, most stores operate on a Dutch auction (described in section **g.** above) basis where the price will continue to drop the longer an item remains in the store. Now you must be able to keep track of not only who owns an item but where it is in the selling cycle. These factors added together make off-the-shelf inventory control programs virtually useless to most secondhand stores.

Wharton, whose company specializes in inventory control systems, realized there was a need for a program to track this information and devoted hundreds of hours to developing and testing a user-friendly software package to meet these unique needs. The result was an easy-to-use, easy-to-customize program which tracks inventory, produces customized contracts, and can even show you trends such as how long certain items take to sell.

It also calculates what an article will be priced at in ten days or ten weeks. "Computerizing has made a world of difference to the smoothness of running my store," says one sporting goods dealer. "I spend less time keeping track of everything, and customers love the fact that I can print them out a forecast so they know exactly what price will be on their bike at any point in the future."

But before you decide to computerize, be sure you weigh the disadvantages carefully. As wonderful as it may sound, there are drawbacks.

The most immediate concern is the bite computerizing will take out of your pocketbook. A customized package will probably run you at least $2,500 (assuming you already have the computer itself) which is a much bigger bite than the shoebox method.

There will be training involved. If you have a high turnover of staff, this can mean many extra hours retraining. As well, if you are not comfortable with computers yourself, the frustration of attempting to keep up-to-date is usually simply not worth the effort. Be sure you are honest with yourself before you set up a fancy system.

3. The devil-may-care method

Sometimes the best inventory control method is no method at all. It may sound like a contradiction to everything we've already said, but sometimes it just isn't worth using a formal, time-consuming tracking system. If you regularly —

(a) stock large numbers of small, low-ticket items such as salt and pepper shakers or crocheted Christmas snowflakes that retail for less than $1,

(b) purchase everything for cash and take no consignment goods whatsoever,

(c) consistently enjoy a fast turnover on your stock,

(d) have an excellent memory for what you paid for an item, or

(e) work alone except for part-time assistants,

you may find you can operate your store without a formal method of tracking each item.

While at first glance this hardly seems like appropriate business practice, the reality is that there are hundreds of dealers who operate this way and still turn a healthy profit every year. These owners invest the time they save on formal inventory control into buying and selling product that will upgrade the overall quality of their store and keep their turnover rate high.

In the end, the choice is yours and will likely depend heavily on your ultimate goals. If your aim is to operate a chain of consignment

Most consignment stores operate on a Dutch auction basis. The price of an item declines by a certain percentage over a period of time — perhaps 10% every two weeks.

Using a computerized inventory control system makes it easy to see trends. For example, knowing that hockey skates take an average of 40 days to sell while in-line skates take only 22 days will help you make more informed buying decisions.

stores located all across your state or province and beyond, our advice is to set up the best inventory control system you can afford as early as possible. If you simply want to enjoy running a single store that will provide you with the income to be independent, a manual method may be simpler in the long run.

Whichever you choose, be meticulous in your record keeping. In the end, an up-to-date tracking method will save you time and money.

i. The case of the missing consignor

At last! You finally sold the miniature red-and-gold gargoyle with the enormous feet and leering eyes that seemed to follow your every move. You pay the consignor and breath a sigh of relief that you'll never have to see his creepy little friend again.

Unfortunately, it sometimes isn't that simple.

1. To phone or not to phone

People will often expect you to do all the follow-up when they consign something with you. As you sell each of their items, they assume you'll let them know. This sounds simple and logical on the surface, but in reality it can rapidly eat up an excessive number of hours out of your day especially when things go wrong. For example, what happens when:

- You get a busy signal five times every day for two weeks in a row?

- The telephone number is no longer in service?

- The telephone number you have is incorrect?

- The answering machine seems to record your message, but you never hear back from the consignor?

- The person who answers the phone says your consignor has just left town for a year long sabbatical in Japan?

Unless they are dealing exclusively in very high-end merchandise, phoning is a service very few secondhand dealers offer.

2. It's up to you, Mr. or Ms. Consignor

"People forget they've left stuff with us all the time," lament many consignment store owners. "We've sold their goods, but they never come back to pick up their money, or even check up on their stuff. We simply don't have the time to call them all."

The most popular way of encouraging consignors to follow up is to make it part of the contract. Be sure you clearly indicate:

    (a) It is the owner's responsibility to contact you when or before their contract expires.

    (b) What will happen to the goods if the owner does not contact you (e.g., the product will be given away, will become the property of the store, or will be used in some other fashion).

Sample #4 shows how to spell out the consignor's responsibilities in your contract. It can also save you future headaches to point this clause out when the consignor first brings in product. Many people don't bother to read "the fine print" and get belligerent when they realize they've made a mistake by not doing so.

3. *To have and to hold forever*

Some secondhand dealers, especially ones who use store credit as part of their payment process, may be willing to keep track of monies owing for longer periods. One paperback book trader recounts a story about a woman who showed up five years after first receiving her credit to claim the credit. During that time she had worked as an English teacher in Japan, married, changed her name, and begun a family. When the dealer looked up her name, sure enough the index card showed she still had almost $100 to use against her purchases. She got to use her credits because her file had never been closed.

While you will likely not want to have and hold for this length of time, you will need to leave an easy-to-follow paper trail documenting every step when you are dealing with abandoned product.

In addition to forgetting, many people simply can't be bothered to collect things they have left at a consignment store. "They've usually already accepted they aren't going to get any money for it," explains a secondhand kids wear consignment dealer. "If their items do sell, it's a nice surprise and if they don't, well, they're no worse off than they were in the first place."

ABC
Clothing
Store

Consignment agreement

1. Consignments are accepted only between the hours of 10 a.m. and 2 p.m. on Tuesday through Friday. Saturdays by appointment.

2. All garments must be cleaned (attach dry cleaning tag if appropriate), pressed, and on hangers.

3. Only articles in style and in excellent condition will be accepted. The Consignee reserves the right to reject any article deemed unsuitable for resale.

4. Consigned goods will be displayed for 60 days. Articles may be claimed at any time during the 60-day period.

5. It is the <u>Consignor's</u> responsibility to contact the store when his or her contract expires. (Check the date on your copy of this contract.) Sale of goods not claimed by or on the expiration date will not be credited to the Consignor's account. Any goods not claimed within 30 days of the expiration of the contract will be donated to charity.

6. The Consignor will receive 50% of the final sale price of their articles.

7. Articles are left in the store at the Consignor's risk. ABC Clothing Store is not responsible for loss due to theft, fire, or any other cause.

Signature: _____

Date: _____

Name (print): _____

Address: _____

_____

Phone: _____

18
Setting your prices

For some retailers, pricing is easy. Take the manufacturer's suggested retail price and double it. In the secondhand business, there is no such thing as a suggested retail price. Every item is unique in terms of age, condition, rarity, and desirability. This is both a source of excitement, for instance, when you buy something for pennies and know you have a buyer who will pay a fortune, and also a few days each year of despair as you realize that you sold a painting for $10,000 less than you could have. Here are some of the factors that go into pricing secondhand goods.

a. Perceived value

Generally, the eventual price of an item is what the purchaser perceives its value to be. Economists use the term "supply and demand" to describe this. In other words, the quantity or supply available of an item, when related to the demand for that item, dictates an appropriate price in the market.

For example, Judy Garland used a few sets of slippers in the *Wizard of Oz*. Although they are only pairs of secondhand shoes, it is a bet they will sell for far more than your old runners. Tons of people would love to have those slippers to wear to a costume party or talk about at dinner or just because they idolized Judy. You'd have to pay someone to wear your old runners.

You must consider what the customer is willing to pay, and what the customer is likely to expect for that price. In other words, does the customer feel that he or she is getting value for money at that price?

b. *Pricing methods*

1. *Traditional industry percent*

In many businesses, a traditional industry percentage figure is applied. For example, retail new clothing stores traditionally apply a 100% markup over cost since they know from experience that this level of markup provides them with a reasonable profit as long as the business is managed properly. Other types of businesses use whatever markup is the norm for their type of business. (See Part I for discussions on pricing specific types of product.)

Alas, it is not possible to use a standard markup on most secondhand items. However, some items are so common that it is possible to have a set buying and selling price. Secondhand computer memory is like this. The price secondhand computer stores will buy or sell it at is usually within a couple dollars of each other.

2. *What the market will bear*

Winging it on pricing goods is probably one of the hardest things to get comfortable with in the secondhand business. It is also one of the more important skills you need to learn. Some of the key factors to consider in establishing individual product prices include:

- Your marketing strategy. You might price Judy's "no-place-like-home" shoes so outrageously that no one would consider buying them, but they would be a great publicity gimmick to have in your store.

- Seasonal or cyclical nature of sales. You may sell all the lawnmowers and garden tools you stock in the spring but sell nothing in the fall. Summer clothes sell in the spring and winter ones in the colder months. Before you stock up, ask yourself if there is a seasonal component to the item's price.

- Nationally advertised prices. It happens occasionally. A used product is sold for more than it will sell for new. This is especially true of computers, where prices fall so fast that a reasonable secondhand price now is more than the new price will be six months from now. If everyone knows the price of the item because it is commonly advertised, you won't be able to sell it without discounting it heavily. Keeping up with nationally advertised prices for new goods is important.

- Your policy on loss leaders — selling below market value (what other people sell the same thing for) is a time-tested way of getting customers in the door. Unfortunately, with secondhand goods, the opportunities to do this are few. It is unusual to find enough of one item you know is in demand that you can sell continuously at a reduced price. Still, the opportunity to buy a box car load of the fashion of the day does happen. One fashion store got a line on a virtually unlimited supply of jeans with slight defects and built a solid business on the customers they lured in by advertising this one product.

3. Competition

You may not be able to ask what an item is really worth because a local competitor is able to get a whack of them cheaply and undercut your price.

4. Your location

Location can play a part. Of course, if the competitor in the above example is a hundred miles from you, your customers may not want to drive all that way to save a few bucks. You can probably sell above your competitor's price.

5. Psychology

Psychology can also play a role in pricing. A $19.99 price tag seems to attract more people to buy than a tag of $20.00. Some retailers avoid ending their prices in even numbers or in 5s, particularly with low-priced items. A $0.29 item is less than a $0.30 one, but it tends to sell more than if it were priced at $0.30 even if customers don't really care about the extra cent. They only think they do.

But don't forget that, for you, the reduction of $0.01 on a $0.30 item is equivalent to $\frac{1}{30}$ or about 3% of gross profit, even though it may not mean much to a customer. Alternatively, increasing a selling price from $0.41 to $0.43 means an increase of about 5% in your gross profit.

6. Economic factors

Economic factors are something you can do little about in pricing, but you should be aware of them. Depressed economic conditions may force you to lower your prices, whereas a healthy economy may allow you to increase them.

If your retail business is located in a company town suffering layoffs, your prices may have to be reduced. If company sales are expanding, your prices can be increased.

Finally, if you are in a tourist location, you may be able to increase your prices during the peak season to compensate for the fact you have to lower them during the off season.

7. Market demand

Products do go out of style and fashion. Be aware of longer term trends developing. Brass used to skip out of secondhand stores, but the pace has slowed some. It is probably fair to say that not one pair of 1960s hip huggers and bell bottoms were sold secondhand during the '80s. If the runways of European fashion are any indication, there may be some demand for them now. Watch for trends developing.

8. Keeping prices within a specified overall price range

Dollar stores sell only items worth a maximum of a dollar or two. Antique stores, junk stores, and secondhand stores all sell secondhand goods. While there are overlaps, they each tend to price their own goods within a relatively narrow range. For example, an old iron might fetch $1 in a junk store but $50 in an antique emporium.

9. Covering costs to provide an adequate profit

The rule of thumb is that the lower the price, the more of something you can sell. Common sense says that the lower the price, the more people can afford to purchase an item. Neophytes to business sometimes mistake all the cash going through their hands for profit. They sell items at or below cost, thinking the volume of sales is an end in itself. Profit is the ultimate goal, so be sure to price your items above your cost and work in enough to cover your other expenses. If an item cannot be consistently sold for enough to contribute to all the other expenses of running your store, drop it or raise the price.

10. Turnover is important

The tendency is to believe that the more you charge, the fewer the number of people wanting to pay the price. Every shop owner must decide whether to wait for the one buyer who will pay the highest price or to sell two of the items at a lower price and lower profit. If you have an unlimited supply of an item, holding out for top dollar makes no sense.

In the secondhand business, many products will be so unique that you will be tempted to hold out for the best price simply because the item is one of a kind. But, unless the item is so unusual that it is a big customer draw or makes your store look fabulous, try to turn it over as quickly as possible.

c. Markup

You have probably heard the term, "it was marked down" or "the markup was over 100%." The markup is the difference between what it costs to purchase and process a product.

The term *markup* is sometimes referred to as gross margin or gross profit, and it is frequently expressed as a percentage of the selling or retail price of the product instead of the cost price.

Because of this, you have to be very careful about using the term *markup*. Be sure you or anyone else involved in calculating markups know whether you are using markup on cost or markup on retail or selling price. The two percentage figures are not the same.

For example, if we expressed a $20 markup as a percentage of a $60 retail price, it would be:

$$\frac{\$20}{\$60} \quad x \quad 100 \quad = \quad 33\%$$

If the item costs $40, the markup as a percentage of the cost would be 50%. Why do both a markup on cost and a markup on retail that yield the same dollars of markup give two quite different percentage figures? The reason is that it is generally initially easier to calculate markup on cost, but to better understand the costs of doing business it is probably easier to understand costs expressed as a percentage of sales or revenue.

On income statements, sales or revenue are usually given the figure of 100% and all other income statement figures are expressed in ratio to 100. For example, if you take the earlier income statement and put percentage figures alongside the dollars, the result would be:

Sale	$60	100%
Cost of sale	$40	67%
Markup	$20	33%
Other costs	$12	20%
Profit	$ 8	13%

The 50% markup on cost now shows as 33% on retail on the income statement. This can be useful information. For example, if you wished to increase profit on sales from 13% to 15%, one way to do this would be to increase the markup on sales from 33% to 35%.

There are always deals out there to make a profit on and the more times you can use a dollar to make a profit, the better off you will be.

The question then is, what would this mean in terms of an increase in markup on cost?

Converting a markup on cost percent to a markup on retail percent is not difficult. Figures can be read from tables such as the one illustrated in Sample #5, or else a hand calculator can quickly do this for you using one or the other of the following two equations:

$$\% \text{ markup on retail} = \frac{\% \text{ markup on cost}}{100\% - \% \text{ markup on retail}}$$

or

$$\% \text{ markup on cost} = \frac{\% \text{ markup on retail}}{100\% + \% \text{ markup on cost}}$$

In our case, we wish to change the markup on retail from 33% to 35%, therefore the markup on cost will change from 50% to:

$$\frac{35\%}{100\% - 35\%} = \frac{54\%}{65\%}$$

and the new selling price of the item will be:

$40 + (54\% \times \$40) = \$40 + \$21.60 = \$61.60$

Can we be sure this is so? Let's calculate the markup on retail to be sure it is 35%:

$$\frac{\$21.60}{\$61.60} \times 100 = 35\%$$

d. Markdown

The opposite of a markup is a markdown. A markdown is a reduction of the retail price because of a sale or other reason. The markdown percent is invariably expressed as a percentage of the retail price and generally does not create the confusion that markups sometimes can. For example, a 10% markdown of the $60 item discussed earlier would result in a price reduction of 10% x $60, or $6, making the new selling price $54.

When you mark down an item and anticipate selling more of that item to compensate, you should be aware of the additional sales required to make up for the markdown or price cut.

For example, if your present markup on retail is 30%, and you cut your prices by 10%, you need to increase your sales by 50% to compensate!

Sample #5
MARKUP CONVERSION CHART

% Markup on cost	% Markup on retail
10.00	9.09
11.11	10.00
20.00	16.67
5.00	20.00
30.00	23.08
33.33	25.00
40.00	28.57
42.86	30.00
50.00	33.33
60.00	33.50
66.67	40.00
70.00	41.18
75.00	42.86
80.00	44.44
90.00	47.37
100.00	50.00

Markdowns should be used only for slow or immovable inventory, to meet unanticipated competition, because your initial price was too high, because of seasonal changes or regular customer-anticipated sales, or for the introduction of new, lower-priced products. In clothing and similar retail stores, style changes can also dictate the need for a markdown.

When deciding on a markdown percent, it is best to establish it at the maximum you are willing to take, for example, 20%. If you offer an initial 10%, followed by a later 10%, this can disturb customers. The next time you offer a markdown sale the potential customer might wait in anticipation of a second markdown. If you don't intend to give one, that sale is lost.

A saying in the retail trade is that the first markdown is the best markdown. In other words, make the first markdown large enough to move the items so inventory is reduced, cash is freed up, and fresh, more profitable inventory can be purchased. Dead or slow moving inventory sitting on shelves or racks costs more and is worth less as time goes by.

e. Loss leaders

Markdowns should be distinguished from loss leaders. Loss leaders are items sold at very appealing prices to generate customer traffic in the hope that these customers, as well as buying the loss leader, will also purchase additional items at regular prices or will return as regular customers in the future.

Loss leaders are normally well-promoted and are offered for a short time. Loss leaders are not generally used for dead or slow moving inventory but rather for regular well-selling stock whose price you decide to reduce for a short period.

f. Rules for not losing your head and wallet about pricing

1. Don't marry your product

At some point everybody buys something that is very special to them. It sits around the store with an outrageous price tag and never sells because the owner's perceived value is higher than anyone else's. Either take the item home as part of your compensation or reduce the price to sell it. The name of the game is to make your dollars earn a profit as many times in a year as possible.

2. *Recognize your mistakes*

Everyone makes buying mistakes and no one enjoys acknowledging the fact. The trick is to recognize and admit it as quickly as possible, get rid of the inventory, and free up the dollars for other purchases.

3. *Don't let personal taste get in the way*

Don't reject products just because you hate them. Velvet paintings come to mind. One man tells of buying a store with a gallery of white-suited Elvises and scantily clad Lolitas all of which promptly went into the trash. When some loyal customers complained, he retrieved them and kept a small inventory of high-turnover, high-profit velvet paintings until something came along that sold better in the space. When you wince making certain kinds of sales, the money you make should be a healing poultice.

4. *Don't price tag everything*

It is advisable not to have price tags on some of the very interesting or unique inventory so your price can be flexible to accommodate the circumstances. Remember the story about the well-dressed customer who pulled up in a BMW and went directly to an old, prominently displayed opthamologist chair? The chair was so heavy, the original owner just wanted the thing out of her basement and the shop owner had paid less than $30. The first words out of the customer's mouth were, "I've got to have this. How much?" Pulling a figure from the air, the shop owner mentioned $2,000, which was too much for the BMW driver. But the counter offer of $1,200, all the money the customer had on him, was quite acceptable.

5. *Pricing unusual items*

The longer you are in the business, the more knowledge you'll have about prices for unusual objects. Even when you don't have a clue and none of your catalogues, books, or contacts can help you, you do develop a second sense about what might be valuable and worth your while researching more thoroughly. Some points to consider:

- Is the item well-built, manufactured, or painted?

- Have you seen one of these before?

- Is it like something you have already sold or know something about?

Marrying a product and refusing to admit mistakes are a deadly combination that have bankrupted more than one businessperson. The good news is that the more mistakes you admit and correct, the easier it becomes.

145

- Can an interested customer shed some light on its value? Occasionally someone will tell you what you have and what it is worth before they buy it.
- Does it look very old or unique? While this is far from foolproof, as replicas become more and more difficult to detect, often your instinct about an item's age is a good tip-off to a great deal.

g. *Evaluate the pricing results*

Pricing is an ongoing problem and you must keep evaluating the results of your pricing policies. Since the costs of your purchases and other business expenses change from time to time, so must your prices to ensure you continue to earn reasonable profits and a satisfactory return on your investment. In particular, check whether you have misjudged your final prices and as a result have inventory that is not moving. At that point, you must seriously consider markdowns.

The evaluation step in pricing is very important. By sensible evaluation you can improve your approach to pricing and increase your future profits.

h. *Will that be cash or credit card?*

Credit cards are a way of life for almost everyone today, especially when it comes to large purchases. From your perspective, though, they are something of a two-edged sword.

1. *The benefits*

Many sales are the result of spur-of-the-moment decisions. "People often walk into the store with no plans to buy anything," says one secondhand furniture dealer. "If I didn't give them the option to use their credit card, I'd lose the sale."

More and more, people simply don't carry more than a few dollars in cash. If you regularly deal in items costing over $50, there's a good chance you will lose sales to customers who use credit cards for the bulk of their purchases.

As well, it's almost impossible to tell whether a check will bounce. If you're dealing with a credit card purchase, authorizing each purchase will at least alert you to many of the basic problems, such as stolen or canceled cards, before the customer walks out of your store with your merchandise.

The credit card option gives you more credibility in many customers' eyes. The perception is that you must be a legitimate, successful business person if you are able to offer this payment option.

2. *The disadvantages*

Processing a credit card transaction may mean more paperwork, especially at the beginning before you have the volume of sales to justify the expense of a swipe machine. It will mean filling out the credit card slip, phoning for authorization, and filing extra documentation when you make your bank deposits. Of course, if you are working in a situation where you must always be mobile, you may never get away from the manual system.

As well, in addition to the initial set up fee, you will pay a percentage of every purchase to the issuing bank. This is known as the merchant discount and may run anywhere from 2% to 5% depending on your sales volume and the strength of your relationship with your banker.

Another thing to consider is that each bank or financial institution offers only one credit card. If you want to use both MasterCard and Visa you will have to open accounts with two separate banks.

Like most other business decisions, you will need to assess the implications to your own situation. There is no one answer for everyone. Many stores selling low-priced items (especially if most product is $10 or less) find credit card sales are not be worth the hassle. But if you deal mainly in high-end product, you should give careful thought before saying no to providing this customer service.

Chapter 25 discusses the risk of credit.

i. *Hey, this isn't what I thought — give me my money back!*

Most secondhand stores maintain an "as is, where is" policy. Fortunately, most people who frequent secondhand stores accept this as the norm. If you do not want the extra hassle of returns, here are three suggestions:

  (a) Have a sign indicating that all sales are final beside your cash register or prominently displayed on the wall behind the cash register.

(b) Have your no-return policy stamped on the receipt or printed directly on your invoices.

(c) Tell the customer the goods are non-refundable before you ring in the sale, especially if it is a large ticket item.

While you will still find people who come back days or even weeks later to try to return product, these simple steps will minimize the chance of confrontation with an irate customer.

Of course, you may elect to allow returns. If you do, you should:

(a) Set a definite time limit. Ten days is a common standard.

(b) Consider whether you want to allow cash refund or store credit only. Many stores, both new and used, reimburse customers for returned product with store credit only.

Bear in mind that there will always be exceptions. One dealer describes a teenage girl who wanted to buy a hand-knitted bed shawl as a gift for her elderly aunt who had just been hospitalized for an indefinite period of time. "I could tell it was an expensive purchase for her, and she was really concerned the aunt wouldn't like the color. Sure we had a no-return policy, but sometimes you've just got to bend the rules a bit."

If you are making an exception, be sure to indicate it on the sales receipt, especially if you have other staff who many not be aware of your decision.

19

Stop thief! Dealing with people on the wrong side of the law

a. Stop thief — Part one

1. Theft is a fact of life

Theft is, unfortunately, a fact of doing business, and no matter how vigilant you are, one day you will discover something missing from your store. If your store is based on outright purchase of product, like all other types of retail sales, you will simply have to calculate the cost of shoplifting into your bottom line.

However, if you carry any consignment goods, you must give careful thought to your policy regarding any items that go missing. Since the product is not yours, you will basically have only two choices when it comes to handling theft:

(a) It's not my product, it's not my problem

Some consignment stores have it written right into the contract consignors sign that if an item is stolen while it is in the store, the store owner is not responsible. Losses due to theft or other casualties including fire or damage are born solely by the owner of the goods. See Sample #4, shown in chapter 17, for an example of this type of agreement.

(b) It was in my store, it's my problem

Other stores feel they must make good on any product lost while in their shop and will pay the consignor what he or she would have received if the item actually sold.

There is no way to say whether one of these methods is right and the other is wrong. The choice is up to you, and you are the only person qualified to say which method works for you. Both have been used by successful secondhand dealers of all types. Just be sure you spell it out in your contract and stick to your own beliefs.

One way to discourage such theft is to train employees to be alert and, in particular, to offer to help customers the moment they enter the store. Businesses that are firm in prosecuting shoplifters may also earn a reputation that discourages potential thieves.

However, despite these measures, more precautions are usually necessary. For example, direct customer access to more expensive items should be limited. Have an employee unlock a display case or rack to remove an item for customer inspection.

Another method that is used effectively by many retailers is to install a device or tag on the item that is difficult, if not impossible, for the customer to remove. If an item leaves the store with the device or tag still attached, it triggers an alarm at any exit and alerts employees to a potential shoplifter. Only if an item is paid for at the sales counter is the alarm device or tag removed. However, while this works with clothing, be careful of destroying the overall appearance of antiques with an ultra modern reminder hanging off the side.

Despite these precautions, shoplifting continues, and it is unfortunate that its cost must be passed on in the form of higher prices to the honest customers.

In the meantime, here are some more tips to help you avoid the problem in the first place:

(a) Keep small, easily pocketed items in a locked display case or cabinet.

(b) While it isn't always possible, try to keep an eye on people browsing through your store. If you are suspicious in any way, make sure the person knows you are watching them. You don't need to actually say anything, but if you follow the person several steps behind, he or she will likely get the point. The downside of this method is that you will sometimes annoy potential customers.

(c)   Avoid setting up your store so there are nooks and crannies you can't see into from the front desk. If it is impossible to avoid this, concave mirrors allow you to see around corners without actually following your customers.

(d)   Install an alarm system and post the stickers announcing the fact in obvious places such as the front window and by the cash register. Sometimes just the fact that a store is monitored is enough to dissuade a potential thief.

(e)   If you are in a particularly high crime area, consider chaining items to an immovable object. This technique is common, in a store which carries, for example, valuable fur or leather coats.

(f)   Post a yard stick to the doorframe to help you get a fairly accurate idea of a thief's height. Of course, this doesn't actually prevent theft, but it will be helpful if you need to file a report with the police. Your local police department should be able to provide you with a stick-on height guide.

There is always a trade off between creating an atmosphere where the customer will feel comfortable and one where you have minimized your risk of theft. Remember that the most secure shop is one with everything chained down and locked up tight. It is also probably going to be a store where few people will return to buy.

2. Creativity among thieves

One thing that's often overlooked is just how creative crooks can be in their approach to crime. Some people believe if crooks were only working on the right side of the law, most of them would be wealthy, well-respected members of society. While the truth of this speculation is open to debate, you can't afford to downplay the truth of thieves' ability to pull off some truly ingenious heists.

One dealer recounts this story about his first confrontation with a serious shoplifter. "It was the middle of summer, hot, and business was slow. There was only one fan on in the store, my partner and I were both uncomfortable, and we'd much rather have been enjoying the beach. So when a very attractive woman came into the store, we were happy to spend half an hour or more chatting with her as she looked at various items throughout the store — anything to relieve the monotony. She asked a lot of questions but she left without buying anything. Ten minutes later, though, she was back. But the big surprise came from the fact that now she was wearing only a *very* skimpy and completely see-through negligee. Needless to say, my

NEVER attempt to stop a robber by using force. A thief who feels threatened may become violent. Your life and health are worth more than trying to be a hero.

151

partner and I were surprised — speechless would actually be a better description."

The woman's plan was to so completely bedazzle the two bored and hormonally challenged young men behind the counter that they would be oblivious to her male partner as he systematically pocketed items preselected during her prior visit. The ruse didn't work, but as the dealer pointed out between gales of laughter, "people will go to some truly amazing lengths — you have to be prepared for anything in this business."

Many would-be thieves are more subtle, however, and it's a mistake to get lulled into thinking you'll always be able to spot one from the way he or she dresses or acts. Here's an example of a smooth operator who did get away with it.

"A young couple came up to my jewelry case a couple of minutes after opening time," says a general goods dealer who successfully worked the flea market circuit for more than ten years. "He was a little guy all dressed in white and wanted to buy a silver chain with a cross for his girlfriend, an absolutely stunning gal. She seemed a bit nervous, but he was so overbearing with her that I didn't think much of it at the time. He had her try several chains of various lengths and weights, and eventually he settled on one worth just under $20. Then he handed me a $100 bill and wanted me to make change. It was the beginning of the day, and I just didn't have enough change yet. He said he'd be happy to wait if one of the booths close by could change the bill. I got the change and kept a close eye on them — at least, so I thought. It wasn't until about 20 minutes later that I realized a $1,600 ring was missing out of one of the showcases."

Thinking about it later, the dealer realized that at one point the man had been standing in such a way that he partially hid his girlfriend. Apparently, she had simply reached behind and taken the ring. "The lure was the $100 bill," explains the dealer. "He faked me out by handing me money worth far more than what he was buying. Of course, by the time I realized it, they were both long gone, so I never did recover the ring." This story did at least have a happy ending: the consignor's insurance covered the loss. But if it's a product you own, you're out the cash.

b. Stop thief — Part two

1. Have I got a great deal for you!

There's an urban legend about a man who leaves his wife and runs away to the Bahamas with his secretary. Several weeks later, he calls his wife, tells her to sell his Porsche, and asks her to send him the money. She's happy to oblige and immediately sells the Porsche — for $50!

You can build your own story around how this myth developed, but as lighthearted and frivolous as it seems, in the secondhand business you need to beware of the deal that seems too good to be true. It usually *isn't* true.

A Porsche for $50 is fairly easy to see as a too-good-to-be-true deal. Unfortunately, it isn't always as simple as it sounds. The following true stories will give you an idea of how creative and credible-sounding people on the wrong side of the law can be.

A general goods dealer received a call from an elderly sounding lady who wanted to sell the contents of her home. Her husband had passed away the previous year, and she was at last ready to get on with her life by moving upstate. He agreed to stop by and make her an offer. Her house had quality furniture — nothing really spectacular but all perfectly saleable. And, to the dealer's delight, there was a large collection of depression glass and three or four original oils that would fetch a good price. They hammered out a deal over tea and home-baked chocolate chip cookies, and the dealer wrote a check on the spot. However, two days later, when he returned with his truck, he was greeted by an entirely different woman — one who was in no way about to let anyone take the contents of her home no matter who they'd paid money to. The identity of the fake owner was never discovered.

Another dealer in fine china and silverware returned to his store elated with the purchase he'd just made — a complete setting for 12 of a hard-to-find pattern. The seller had been a tough one, and it had taken almost two hours to negotiate the final price. To his annoyance, his partner was less enthusiastic about his recent triumph, insisting it sounded too good in spite of the two hours of haggling. Sure enough, when they called the police, they discovered that the silverware was stolen. The thief had used the heat of the negotiating process to blind the dealer to what he was really buying.

And finally, here's an interesting twist on the same theme. A man dressed in casual but conservative clothing stalled his motorbike in front of a used goods store. It was soon obvious to everyone inside that this was not the first time he'd had trouble with the bike. First he stamped in frustration, then he kicked the offending machine. Before long he was screaming that he'd sell "this piece of junk" to anyone stupid enough to give him $100 for it. The store owner eventually couldn't resist the challenge. He took $100 out of the till and made an offer. The owner of the bike seemed a bit taken back at first, but finally agreed to sell it.

After he'd phoned a cab and been driven away, the new owner took a closer look at the bike. It was running rough, although it didn't seem as if it would take too much effort to fix. But something nagged at the new owner. It was just a "bad feeling," but he took the precaution of wheeling the bike into his underground parking. The area was well lit and secured with a ten-foot chain link fence.

Next morning when the owner arrived to start working on the bike, he discovered someone had attempted to break into the lockup area. Although the thief wasn't able to get through the fence, he or she was able to unscrew several of the smaller parts and remove the headlight. The moral of the story according to this dealer is that if someone attempts to sell something to you too cheaply, they may be planning to come back and retrieve it later.

2. *Saying no to stolen goods*

If you think someone is trying to sell you stolen property do not *under any circumstances* buy it. Not only do you open yourself to a criminal charge for selling stolen goods, but if they are confiscated (which they often are) you lose the goods plus the cash you paid out for them. If you must, invent an excuse. "I'm sorry, we just took a consignment of ten similar items and we really can't handle any more at this time" works fine in most circumstances.

As soon as the person is out of the store, phone the police with a complete description. If you can, take down his or her license plate number as well. Once you've made your report, write everything you can remember down in a notebook or on a paper you can file away. As vivid as the impression is at the moment it happens, memory fades quickly. The more details you can jot down, the easier it will be if you need to follow up on the report later. It's unfortunate that most frequently your report won't result in an arrest, but the more information you can give, the greater the chance it will.

Here are some things which may alert you to a possible problem:

- The person appears nervous and in a hurry. He or she may be constantly glancing out the window or at his or her watch.

- The items the person is selling don't seem to go together. For example, a person who brings in a bunch of nearly new romance novels, several out-of-date physics textbooks, and a couple of sing-along music books with movie themes from the 1950s.

- The person doesn't seem to know much about what he or she is selling (e.g., someone is trying to sell you an extensive stamp collection without knowing what a philatelist is).

- There's a conflict between the personality type and the goods he or she is trying to sell. A 16-year-old wearing leathers and a nose ring isn't a very likely candidate to be selling a set of expensive silverware or a delicate Oriental jade carving.

- There are no stories or personal history that go with the articles. Many people will say things like, "I really hate to part with this because . . ." or, "This was given to me by my ex-mother-in-law and I can't wait to finally get rid of the damned thing."

- The person will only accept cash. Thieves generally aren't interested in checks because they don't have bank accounts. While cash payment is the most common way to pay for product, be wary if the person insists on cash only.

- The person may accept the first price you offer them without bargaining even if it's well below the going rate.

- Your intuition is shrieking at you. Don't ignore the importance of paying attention to your instincts. Any one of the above criteria sometimes means nothing more than a person who's uncomfortable or nervous around people or who is very unhappy about selling off some favorite memento. On the flip side, many successful thieves are just as cool, calm, and sophisticated as anyone you'd expect to meet at your local business luncheon. If you have nothing more than a gut feeling, you're often best to listen to it — it's amazing how often it's the most accurate indicator of all.

Trust your instincts when it comes to assessing a person who may be trying to sell you stolen property.

c. Remember the overall picture

Before you start believing that secondhand stores are all the victims of grand larceny on an hourly basis, think of the bright side. Most secondhand dealers report that no matter what product they sell, the rate of theft seems to be relatively low compared to other shops.

Perhaps, as one dealer points out, it's greed. "After all," she asks, "why would any thief in their right mind steal a bunch of used books? If you're a crook there are lots of more attractive things to steal in stores that carry new product."

But more likely it's to do with the clientele. Dealers in all types of secondhand sales mirror the sentiments of this dealer who says, "People who come into a secondhand store have a different mentality to start off with. They tend to be very easy-going, relaxed, and honest. And that goes a long way to making up for some of the other problems."

20
Managing your employees

For many new business owners, working with employees is one of the toughest parts of the job. Reassure yourself; nobody has the magical answer. Everyone suffers from hiring mistakes, difficult employees, and turnover. Nobody gets it right all the time. However, there are some tips you can keep in mind to improve the likelihood of hiring and developing winners.

a. Hiring

(a) *Make the hiring process as objective as possible.* If you ask most managers why they hired a particular person, you'll get a totally subjective response — "I like the person." Personal reactions to an individual, instincts, and intuition are a valid contribution to the process. But, it's also helpful to add some reasonably objective information and data. The application or résumé submitted by a candidate should give you some idea of what skills the applicant will bring to the job.

(b) *Allow adequate time, and interview in an appropriate environment.* Conducting interviews standing in a corner of your store while rushed and preoccupied with other matters is no way to make hiring decisions. You need to schedule interview appointments, allow at least 20 to 30 minutes for each interview, and conduct the interviews in a private, comfortable place.

(c) *Consider as many applicants as possible.* One of the classic hiring mistakes is jumping at the first apparently qualified candidate. Small business owners often hire only when they urgently need an employee and are under considerable pressure to fill the opening. This kind of pressure does not often facilitate good judgment. If at all possible, give yourself at least a few weeks to make your selection decisions and, during that time, interview as many available candidates as possible.

(d) *Always check references thoroughly.* In the convenience store industry, where employee theft is extraordinarily common and costly to employers, there actually are career criminals — employees who go from job to job for the purpose of stealing cash and merchandise from their employers. Even though this is a well-known fact in that industry, these career criminals can continue getting hired after getting fired for stealing, simply because most managers never check their references!

Many managers assume that the references provided by an applicant will include only approving comments or the applicant wouldn't have provided them — but this is not true. Checking references and conversing with previous employers can and does reveal everything from outright deception to serious behavioral deficiencies on the part of the applicant.

Sample #6 is a form you can use when checking employee references.

b. Keeping employees

The person who started work this morning is as close to a model employee as you'll ever get. From there, in most businesses, the employee's interest, enthusiasm, commitment, and performance generally erodes — from model to merely adequate to, finally, unacceptable. This process is at least partly the employer's fault.

Day One is your opportunity to take your model employee and set him or her up to stay that way. This is when you need to really invest time with the new person, cover your business philosophy, clearly outline your expectations, teach, establish rapport, and

APPLICANT REFERENCE CHECK

Applicant's name: _____

Reference business called: _____

Individual at that business spoken to: _____

Employment dates applicant gave on application: _____

Dates verified by reference: ___Yes ___ No ___ Not applicable

Position held: _____

Basic duties: _____

_____

_____

_____

Was applicant ever promoted? If so, to what position: _____

_____

Was applicant ever given a merit raise? _____

Why did applicant leave? _____

Would applicant be considered for re-hire in the future? ___Yes ___ No

If no, why not: _____

_____

On a scale of 1 to 10, rate the applicant's:

Punctuality	1	2	3	4	5	6	7	8	9	10
Integrity	1	2	3	4	5	6	7	8	9	10
Cooperation with others	1	2	3	4	5	6	7	8	9	10
Overall job performance	1	2	3	4	5	6	7	8	9	10

Other comments:_____

_____

_____

_____

_____

_____

acquaint the new person with other employees. Most managers give new employees just a few minutes of instructions and then throw them into the water to sink or swim on their own. It's much smarter to do the opposite and really work with the new person.

For more tips on hiring, see *A Small Business Guide to Employee Selection*, another title in the Self-Counsel Series.

1. Training

It is a lot easier to remember some tedious filing chore if you know those files are used regularly for some real purpose.

The manager's frustrated refrain, "But I told them that!" can be heard every minute of every work day somewhere in your town. But "telling them" just isn't enough. Follow the six steps to effective employee training:

(a) *Explain what is to be done and why.* Under the daily pressure to get things done, you may be tempted to dictate what is to be done giving only the explanation "because I said so, and I'm the boss." This is a short-sighted approach. Employees are not robots, content to mindlessly carry out tasks that are meaningless to them. Without knowing why they are doing something, they cannot feel any enthusiasm for the task nor feel a part of a team that is accomplishing something.

An employee who understands why a task is necessary may very well come up with some more efficient way of doing the job, saving you time and money. Such initiative is impossible if the employee simply performs the task without knowing its purpose. Explain why the job is important; you will have a happier employee and you may reap financial benefits as well.

(b) *Explain each major point or step of the task.* Training should be delivered in an organized, memorable manner.

(c) *Demonstrate.* If you are teaching something that can be demonstrated or role-played, take the time to do it.

(d) *Observe.* If possible, have the trainee show you what he or she has learned, while you observe.

(e) *Critique.* After observing the trainee's demonstration, praise what was done well and correct what needs to be done differently or better.

(f) *Follow up.* Just because the trainee manages to do the task once does not mean he or she will perform that way forever. A common managerial experience is "Monday morning amnesia" — people who seem to have forgotten their jobs over the weekend! Periodically you need to "inspect what you expect."

2. Motivating employees

Tens of thousands of people walk away from jobs every day. The idea of hanging onto a job no matter what no longer operates in our society. To keep good employees and encourage them to do their best work for you, you need to be concerned with what *they* want from the job, not just what you want from them.

In his book *Reinventing the Corporation*, futurist John Naisbitt suggested ten things that employees really want from their jobs:

(a) To work for people who treat me with respect

(b) Interesting work

(c) Recognition for good work

(d) Opportunity to develop new skills

(e) To work for people who listen to ideas on how to do things better

(f) A chance to think for myself rather than just carry out instructions

(g) To see the end result of my work

(h) To work for efficient managers

(i) A job that is not too easy

(j) To be informed

Your motivational formula should include: clear communication of expectations, standards, policies, and procedures; public and personal recognition of a job well done; and monetary and non-monetary rewards.

For more information on this subject, look for *Motivating Today's Work Force*, another book in the Self-Counsel Series.

c. *Firing*

In most cases, employees performing unsatisfactorily know they should be let go long before they are. The other employees know it, and you know it before you finally do it. One bad apple can spoil the whole barrel, and letting a problem persist with no reason to expect change is a very bad lapse of control.

When a problem exists, take immediate and decisive action. You can and should first try to discuss the matter with the person. If

If you are firing an employee of the opposite sex, you may want a witness in the room with you.

agreement can be reached concerning correction and improvement, it should be documented. If improvement does not happen as agreed, do not hesitate to follow up immediately.

This is not the time to be petty or spiteful; your job is to solve the problem with as little muss and fuss as possible. It's best to be relatively gracious and polite, but firm.

You should make a statement to the rest of your team concerning the termination, without being overly critical or nasty about the terminated employee. Reassure the others that it was a decision based on job performance and related issues rather than a sign of other layoffs or terminations to come.

21
Get 'em in the door

Advertising is an expensive trial and error endeavor. Yet the second-hand store that goes without it is missing an important opportunity to strengthen its customer base. It is a rare retail store that cannot benefit from advertising.

The objective of advertising is to increase sales. To advertise efficiently you must know how much sales increase for every dollar you spend on advertising. To run an effective advertising campaign you need to —

(a) choose a goal for your advertising campaign,

(b) select and evaluate the most effective advertising medium,

(c) create an eye- or ear-catching ad to draw the prospect's attention, and

(d) evaluate the return on your advertising dollar.

If sales do not increase, change the ad content, the medium, or the product you are advertising and try it again. For a small, newly opened secondhand store with a restricted budget, professional help to design an advertising campaign is probably a waste of money. The fees you would pay to a consultant could most likely be better spent trying new ads.

a. Choose a goal

Are you new to the neighborhood and want people to know you are there? Do you have an unlimited number of replica 18th-century brass ship lanterns to sell? Are you looking for consignment goods to sell? Before you start any campaign, you must determine exactly what you want to accomplish. Advertising without a specific goal is throwing away money.

b. Selecting your advertising medium

Selecting your advertising medium is a sure-fire method for determining ahead of time if a particular medium works for your type of secondhand store. Call a secondhand store in a distant city and ask where it advertises. You will be surprised how much other store owners will usually tell you about their methods and what works. When you are about to select a paper or station to advertise with in your own city, ask that publication or station for a list of past secondhand advertisers. Call and ask each store's opinion of the results of their ads.

1. Radio and television

Television has the advantage of being able to create images for the viewer. If you have terrific fashions, you can let the audience know with a montage of some of your products flashing across the screen in seconds.

Radio and television ads are expensive and require a sizable commitment just to see if they work. Television advertising is usually closed to all but a few large firms that can afford thousands of dollars for production costs of a commercial, in addition to the cost per commercial spot. Since you may have to try several different time slots or even change television stations or commercials before you find the right combination, your budget for a television campaign must be substantial. A few late-night ads will not make the ad pay. You must risk comparatively large sums of money before you know if you have a winner.

Still, there are secondhand stores that advertise on television and swear by the results. All these companies have either multiple outlets or are very large.

Generally speaking, radio is a bust for secondhand goods but depending on the area, it might be possible to generate some sales this way.

If you are going to advertise on radio, negotiate hard for good rates. Except for the most popular stations, most stations will give you a deal to entice you to try their service. Radio is sold in "spots" that can be 10, 15, 30, or 60 seconds long. Stations usually discourage the shorter ads since they require more effort to schedule for less money. The cost of a spot depends on when the ad is run, which in turn depends on how many listeners usually tune in during that time of day. The most expensive times are during the drive to and from work. You can put together a mix of different spots, but the more you vary the time, the harder it is to figure out the most efficient periods in which to concentrate your ads for a future campaign. Production costs of the ad are usually included in the cost of a series of advertisements if the commercial is not too elaborate.

2. Print advertising

Print advertising means you can create your own ads with comparative ease. A simple text ad may be all you need and the magazine or newspaper will probably set the type for free. Print advertising is also low risk compared to radio and television. With a small budget you can get a good feel for whether to continue with the tactics you have now or change one of the variables in your advertising.

(a) Newspapers

Newspapers are a common means of advertising retail outlets. The biggest advantage to newspapers is their flexibility. You can use graphics or text in different-sized ads to get your message across.

It is also comparatively easy to change your ad as the situation changes. If demand is higher than you expected and you run out of stock, simply cancel the ad. Or in a day you can fashion an ad to advertise something else.

Don't overlook small community newspapers in favor of larger dailies. These smaller papers are not only cheaper but may target your ad to the group of people you want to reach. It is a waste of money to reach a large circulation that is too far away for you to do business with.

Newspapers also have a price structure that provides special contract rates. By committing your company to buying a certain amount of space over a certain period of time, you can reduce your per insertion cost. Normally the paper wants you to commit to a minimum number of lines of classified advertising or inches of display space per year. Work out what this will mean on a weekly basis to see if you can come anywhere near the required amount. Contracts can lower your cost of advertising by a significant amount if you complete the contract. Some contracts are so loosely drawn that you can opt in and out of the contract rate as you like. Others are more stringent. Be sure to read and understand your obligations.

When you are choosing a newspaper to advertise in, consider the following:

(a) Does the newspaper's circulation area overlap the area in which you concentrate your marketing? Unless you want to develop new areas and have created a campaign to support it, advertising to a far-off place might be a waste of time.

If a particular paper with a wide circulation seems to be pulling well despite many of its readers being outside your normal marketing area, consider expanding your advertising to include it.

(b) Can you afford a series of ads? One ad may not be enough to test the efficacy of a particular newspaper. Many advertising gurus advocate a series of ads to truly test a market. There is some truth to the idea that advertising is cumulative. A series of ads aimed at the same people is more effective than an ad done once but aimed at different groups, but not everybody has the cash to risk a series.

(c) Is the newspaper read by the people you want to reach? Do you want a biker clientele? Students? The limousine set? Advertise in publications that cater to them. You have wasted your money if you don't try to target the people who are most likely to shop in your store.

(b) Magazines

Magazine advertising is expensive and may not be timely enough to be of much value to you. It may be several weeks or months between the time you place your fashion ad and the time the magazine hits the newsstands. Monthly magazines may not be on sale until long past the expiration date of any super deals you advertise.

Offsetting these big disadvantages is the fact that people may read magazines long after a newspaper is tossed in the garbage.

c. Creating effective print advertising

1. Pick the product to advertise

The first step in creating effective print advertising is choosing which product you want to advertise. Try to tap into a market made up of people who may be interested in what you have to offer. With winter approaching, try winter coats, or in the fall, sell all those obsolete cheap computers as word processors to students. Common sense will narrow the field for you. A lot of this is guesswork in the beginning, although you can get tips from what other stores like yours advertise consistently.

Usually secondhand store advertising is about particular kinds of product. Emphasis in an ad may be on a specific shelf or dresser or computer that is representative of what you specialize in.

Occasionally store ads emphasize something else such as special expert knowledge about collectibles or fashion or convenient location, stability, and dependability. In general, product specific marketing is recommended to bring in the type of customers you want. So many businesses promise expert advice or good service that the public often sees this as meaningless puffery.

2. Create your ad

Unless you have tons of money, skip the "feel good" image ads. Instead, briefly tell the reader exactly what your special offer is with prices. The ad must be short and to the point.

One popular and effective way to communicate information is to name one of your products using a single headline, possibly accompanied by a picture prominently displaying the product. Of course, you will also want to include the price. Always show your address in large bold type at the very bottom of the ad so people do not have to search for it. Phone numbers should be included only if you want to accept phone calls. Your company name and logo lend credibility to the ad and help people associate your secondhand store with your specialty.

For your first ad, pick a product you have lots of and one you think might be popular with the people you want as customers. Try a two- or three-inch display ad with a large headline, a prominent dollar price, and a big name and address. The words "from" in small letters might precede the dollar value if you are offering a range of prices. Make sure it is an excellent price compared with other ads for the same product.

You can try exactly the same ad in the classified section or alter it slightly to save money. By downsizing it to a regular line ad, you can pay a fraction of the price of a display ad and you may get just as many customers. Try each of these tactics and compare the response.

3. Choose the right vehicle

Advertise where everyone else advertises — because that is where customers have been educated to look. Advertising secondhand goods in the food section of a newspaper is probably not effective. First, go to the library and get copies of every magazine and newspaper that cover your area. Look for other advertisers, not just secondhand dealers, who might be selling the same product you are thinking of advertising. Call them to see if the paper or magazine gets customers for them. Even new goods advertisers may have some interesting feedback.

When you have selected a candidate or two, contact them for rate information. Try to negotiate a better rate as a first-time advertiser, and then place your ad.

d. Evaluating the response

An easy test is to assume that everyone who purchases the item in a week saw your advertisement. With the money you made, did you cover the cost of the ad? If the answer is no under this ideal condition, your ad is probably a bust.

The first indications an ad has "pull" is that the phone starts ringing more often or you get more customers coming in. However, this is not the measure of the success of the ad. It is a limited measure of how well you created your ad or how well you chose your vehicle. People obviously saw the ad and are curious enough to want to know more. Ask the staff to keep tallies of customers who come in as a result of reading your ad. This serves as an early warning system for bad ads. If there are few calls or drop ins, you may want to cancel the ad early and save your cash.

Ask yourself if doubling or tripling the number of sales will change the situation. Every ad needs to be given a chance to perform, but if two or three times the current volume of calls will not make a difference, you definitely have a dud.

Even if there are numerous enquiries, later analysis may show that not one person bought anything. Do not mistake action for results. Every time the phone rings or a customer drops in to ask about the product, it costs you and your staff time to serve that person. If no sales result, you are losing not only advertising dollars but staffing dollars too.

To evaluate an ad, you must have a system in place that records where every sale came from. Every time a sale is made, the sales person must be sure to ask them, "Where did you hear about this shelving unit?" and then record the answer. Keep a small notebook by the cash register to record the date, the product, and how the customer heard about your store. The manager is responsible for ensuring every sale of the item you are advertising has a corresponding source recorded.

Each advertising vehicle must be coded and all the sales staff must know the codes. For instance, customers from referrals could be given the code *W/M* for *word of mouth*; customers who have dealt with you before coded *R* for *repeat or drop in*; and newspaper ads coded with the newspaper's name in abbreviated form, such as *Metro* for the major daily. Make the codes easy. Stay away from cryptic references and numbering your sources. Your staff will never remember them and will not record them accurately.

By adding up the dollar amount in sales that each ad generated, you can get a measure of how well the ad is pulling. An ad generating less in sales than twice the cost of the ad should be looked at critically. It probably did not make you money and you should watch to see if sales from it pick up as the ad continues. An ad that covers only its own cost lost you money.

Ads that pull in customers but do not result in sales could indicate several things. Maybe one of your competitors advertised a much better price than you did on the product you chose. Lower your price and try again or wait until your competitor stops advertising that price. Or it may be too early in the season to make sales. People may be just window shopping. Try the ad later in the season.

By keeping careful records, you can intelligently budget your advertising dollars and avoid waste. Micro-managing your advertising budget does pay off. To let an ad run until you get a "feel" for whether the ad works is foolish. If the product you picked requires a lot of work per inquiry, and your sales people are busy fielding queries, it may feel like the ad is doing its job. But, in fact, it might be just sucking up your cash and time.

1. *Helpful hints for print advertising*

Every magazine and newspaper and, for that matter, every locale, is different. You will have to experiment with the advertising opportunities in your area. Experienced advertisers offer these suggestions:

(a) Watch what other advertisers do time after time. This may give you a clue about what makes a successful ad or advertising campaign.

(b) There is a cumulative effect in advertising. If you advertise now, you may still be getting some response from the ad months later. However, do not let the cumulative effect fool you into thinking an ad might still work if it did not pull anything the week it ran. A dud ad now is a cumulative dud ad, too.

(c) For the same budget, run smaller ads more frequently rather than opting for larger ads fewer times.

(d) Ads under an inch-and-a-half tend to get lost in display advertising. Ads over a quarter page do not have double the pulling power of ads half that size.

(e) Ads under four lines do not pull well in classified sections.

(f) Always tell your entire sales staff exactly what the ads you have placed are about before the ad goes in. Your credibility goes out the window when a potential customer calls about the super special deal you advertised and no one knows what the customer is talking about. There should be no exceptions to this rule.

(g) Never run an ad without checking that it is properly placed and correctly worded. If you cannot get a copy of the magazine or newspaper or a clipping faxed to you on the day the ad first runs, ask your sales staff if they are getting calls from the new ad.

(h) Know what your competition is offering. It does no good to have side-by-side ads offering the same French doors when your price is $50 higher. There will be times when you just cannot advertise because your competitors have a better deal than you do. If this happens all the time, concentrate your marketing efforts on other products that will generate better results or advertise in different newspapers or magazines.

(i) Don't forget newsletters. The best way to advertise to a very specialized group of customers, for example, military paraphernalia collectors, is to attend shows directed at them. Some of these shows do direct mailings to potential customers or have newsletters. You might be able to advertise in them.

(j) Seasonal considerations and timing may play a part in your advertising for your area. For instance, advertising on long weekends reaches fewer people because many of them take the opportunity to take a mini vacation. Days on either side of the weekend are dead too, especially in the summer. The week between Christmas and New Year's can be very slow, especially if Christmas is in the middle of the week. To save money, you may want to cancel all your advertising. Experiment a bit.

There may also be a sales cycle that you shouldn't ignore. Sometimes no matter how big a budget you spend, you can't generate many sales. The smart thing to do is to save your cash. Unfortunately, it may take several cycles before you identify these slow cycles. Keeping an advertising diary has proved helpful to some businesses. In conjunction with a month-by-month sales report, you can pinpoint cycles early and the money can be put to better use.

(k) In situations where your advertising options are limited, such as in a very small town, do not waste your time on advertising. Personal contact is more effective.

(l) Finding your first consistently winning ad may take some time. Do not be discouraged. It does take a lot of work. Once you have your first really successful ad, it is easier to do the trial and error. No matter how successful your ads may become, do not stop working your advertising budget hard and trying new approaches.

e. *Other advertising options*

1. *Co-op advertising*

If you are selling a mix of new and secondhand goods, for instance antiques and replicas, some suppliers will share advertising costs with you if you are running an ad that exclusively advertises their product. They may put up as much as 50% of the cost of the ad. To make this an attractive idea for suppliers, you need a well-thought-out approach. Know the kind of ad you want to run, and the number of times it will run. Generally, suppliers do not require a written proposal, but it is advisable for you to get confirmation in writing that they will pick up the agreed-on percentage of the bill.

2. *Piggyback on someone else's marketing*

Look for opportunities to share the costs of reaching your audience with someone else. A prime example is the firm that pays part of a bank's statement mailing cost each month and in exchange inserts a blurb of their own in the envelope. Good opportunities are few. If another party is interested in your idea, you must first determine if the customers you will be reaching are the kind of people who would normally buy from you.

3. Direct mail

Unless you have a very well-qualified list of prospects, spend your budget slowly and carefully, testing as you increase your mailing size.

Direct mail and handbills are very expensive and time-consuming. A direct-mail campaign including postage, handling and stuffing, production of the ad, and the waste of undelivered pieces, may run you as much as a $1 per piece delivered. On top of that is the time or money it costs to produce great copy. Still, if you have a list of collectors of, say, depression glass, direct mail can be a money spinner.

Handbills and flyers on car windshields or in mailboxes do not normally produce positive results. The exception seems to be when you stick to a small geographic area and emphasize your close location. This approach works best at the beginning of your business when you want to introduce yourself to customers in your immediate area.

4. Your prospect list

A prospect list is an easy system all secondhand businesses should consider using. As customers come in looking for particular things, take down their name, phone number, and a description of what they want. Keep the notebook near the cash register so all your employees have access to it. There is nothing as pleasing as making a purchase, calling a customer, and selling an item for a tidy profit within hours of buying it.

This is a guaranteed method of making sales. Of course, the temptation is to buy only what those customers are looking for. This can work as long as the item is of interest to many people. You do not want to buy a strange item that only one person has ever expressed interest in and never be able to resell it.

5. Directories

Listing in a directory has its advantages and disadvantages. An advertisement in a directory may be around for a year, which means your ad cannot list prices. Nor can you change the ad if your business or marketing thrust changes. You are limited to messages that might amount to puffery in the public's mind or to listing only the products you normally stock.

172

As an example, the Yellow Pages reaches a tremendous number of people, but advertising rates are expensive. Many secondhand dealers swear by the Yellow Pages as an effective advertising tool, but some do not. Check to see who advertises consistently before you put your money down. The library has copies from past years, so you can see who actually is willing to pay those premium rates year after year. Or you might get some information by calling advertisers directly.

6. Signage

Many businesspeople don't even think of using signs as an advertising medium, but you shouldn't neglect this low-cost or free opportunity to advertise on the business's own building, windows, delivery vehicles, or company cars.

f. Final considerations

It is common during economic downturns for managers and owners to look for places to cut expenses. The one place you should never cut is your advertising budget. Instead of cutting, you might even consider increasing your expenditure. Think of your advertising dollar as an investment, not an expense.

Probably the most important aspect of advertising is to carefully analyze and know your market so you can then use the most appropriate mediums. In other words, who are your customers? The better you know your market, the more cost effective your advertising will be since it can be directed more specifically at those people. Don't try to advertise everywhere. Put your money into one or two kinds of advertising. Spreading your budget too thin will detract from your impact.

Once an advertising strategy has been designed, it should be maintained continuously and consistently, although this does not mean that, where the need arises, some occasional special advertising cannot be added. Repetitive advertising (a minimum of six times is recommended) is also necessary to be effective for most advertising media.

Remember that no amount of advertising will overcome bad pricing, a bad choice of products to sell, or rotten service. Advertising is an important piece of your marketing effort, but not all of it.

For more information on this subject, you might want to refer to *The Advertising Handbook*, another title in the Self-Counsel Series.

22

Keeping the customers satisfied

The most important, productive, valuable asset you will ever possess in business is your customer. Everything else is replaceable. Businesses that mistreat or undervalue their customers always fail eventually. Some may look successful for a while. Some will hang on longer than others. But ultimately they all die.

Once you have spent money to establish yourself in a convenient location, to ensure your store is a good place to do business, to hire staff to look after customers, to stock your inventory with good products, and to advertise to bring customers to you, don't lose those customers because of poor customer service practices. Your customers are far more valuable to you than just anyone out in the street — they have already indicated interest in buying by answering your ad or entering your store — so taking an "Oh, well, there are always more fish in the ocean" approach is just plain dumb. All your efforts up to this point have been directed at getting customers to come into your store or answer your ad. What you have to do now is back up your ads and promises with some service and you will have regular customers instead of prospective customers.

a. Meeting and exceeding expectations

For customer service that will be memorable for all the right reasons, you have to understand all your customers' expectations and outperform them.

Here are the factors that control a customer's expectations:
- The customer's needs
- The customer's desires
- The business's advertising
- The market or competition
- What the customer knows about quality
- The business's externals — location, signage, etc.
- The customer's past experience
- The business's reputation

b. Making money from referrals

One great result of customer service exceeding expectation is positive word-of-mouth advertising. It is better to gain a customer as a result of referral from another established, satisfied customer than through any form of commercial advertising. Here are some of the reasons why.

(a) Lower marketing cost. Obviously, it costs less to get a customer through a referral than to get one through advertising. In many cases, it's free or virtually free.

(b) Less price resistance. Customers referred by satisfied customers come with a certain level of pre-established trust. They are predisposed to buy. And they'll be less resistant to price than new customers attracted by advertising.

(c) More referrals. The customer who comes to your store because a friend recommended you is much more likely to, in turn, refer your store to someone else than is the advertising-generated customer. Many businesses have endless chains of referrals: Mary refers Bob who refers Janet ... and so on.

For these reasons, it is worth your while to work at stimulating referrals.

Often, moving from adequate/good customer service, which creates few or no referrals, to exceptional customer service, which dramatically exceeds customer expectations and creates many referrals, involves "little things." These little things can make a big difference in just about any business. Here are some tips for getting maximum positive word-of-mouth advertising and referrals:

- Make it a marketing and management priority.
- Become a serious student of word-of-mouth advertising.
- Define your customers' expectations. Keep amending and adding to the list as your understanding of your customers grows.
- Set up a plan to consistently exceed those expectations.
- Look for new ways to exceed customer expectations.
- Ask your customers, through surveys, questionnaires, conversation, etc., what they need, want, like, and don't like.
- Measure the success of your word-of-mouth advertising. Keep track of the number of referrals you get in total and the percentage of your customers who do refer.

c. Handling complaints

There will inevitably be times when your business fails to meet customer expectations. If you are lucky, this will result in complaints. Yes — if you are *lucky* you will get complaints. Most unhappy customers do not complain; they simply walk away and resolve never to spend their money at your business again. Then, you have lost not only a customer, but also all the potential customers that the lost customer will warn away. You have also lost the chance to learn from the situation and improve your business so the problem does not occur again.

Customer complaints give you one of your best opportunities to go beyond the ordinary in customer service and win over the customer. Unfortunately, too many businesses do not see it that way. They think of complaints as a bother or an unjustified attack on their business. Don't make this mistake.

For some perverse reason, we all tend to gripe about our unhappy consumer experiences more than we tell others about our satisfactory experiences. The horror stories are more fun to tell. Telling them lets us vent our frustrations and irritation. So, if you alienate a customer, you can count on dozens of people hearing about it. One unhappy customer can do damage that a dozen satisfied customers cannot mend.

If your customer does complain, you have the chance to make it right. Send that customer away convinced you are the best business in town, and resolve the problem in your business.

Of course, there are times when the customer is actually wrong, so outrageously wrong that your only choice is to sacrifice him or her and all those he or she may poison. Bill Cosby once said, "I'm not sure what the secret of success is — but I do believe the secret of failure is trying to please everybody." But preventing the creation of a bad-will ambassador must be a top priority.

Prevention and effective management of complaints is a marketing function.

d. Your complaint resolution and prevention program

As a marketing function of your business, you need both a complaint prevention program and a complaint correction, fast-response program. Complaint resolution steps vary widely from one type of business to another. Here are some general points you should consider when drafting your policy for handling complaints:

(a) Don't argue with the customer. When you or your employee is listening, writing down facts, and accepting a customer complaint, the temperature of the conflict is not getting worse, and may get better. Often, the complainer will blow off a lot of steam, wind down, and become reasonable all of his or her own accord. But any argument only serves to fan the flames, send the temperature through the roof, and heighten the difficulty of finding a resolution.

(b) The person facing the complainer or taking the complaint call should have as much authority as possible, so he or she can assure the customer that something will be done. In some businesses, there are set parameters staff members can operate within to resolve complaints on their own.

(c) The faster the complaint can be resolved, the better. A waiting customer can become worked up and ready for a fight. By having a fast response and resolution plan for your business, you eliminate this part of the problem.

(d) The decision not to resolve a complaint should never be made without the owner's or top manager's knowledge.

(e) When you do resolve a complaint reasonably and amicably, if you want to keep that person as a customer, it's perfectly appropriate to continue soliciting his or her business by mail, by phone, or in person.

For more about customer service, see *Keeping Customers Happy,* another title in the Self-Counsel Series.

23
Publicity

There is no doubt about it, the secondhand business has some characters. In one city, two brothers had competing secondhand stores next to each other and provided theater for passersby with their constant bickering. The first brother would place a rocking chair out in front of the building with a price tag on it. Immediately the second brother would come over and loudly tell anyone who was passing all about the chair's flaws. "Overpriced! Overpriced and ugly! For that price you could buy two of mine." And then he would promptly pull out his rockers.

The first brother would saunter over and begin his harangue about the second brother's products. Their attacks were loud and venomous and attracted the local television stations. Business improved. People came just to see what would happen and, of course, the rival siblings would put on a show. They also sold a lot of secondhand goods.

You guessed it. They had staged it all.

In Vancouver, B.C., the flamboyant "Captain" takes television audiences with him as he wears Martian costumes or hardly anything at all (it's startling to see him prance across the screen in a grass skirt) to places as far away as the South Pacific. What does this have to do with promoting his secondhand store? Nothing, except he lassos your attention and always delivers his message about the great deals he has. He has expanded from one small store to several.

Publicity stunts used to be the norm in promoting products, businesses, and even Hollywood celebrities. There were publicity agents who got paid for dreaming up and implementing these stunts. Many of the entries in *The Guinness Book of World Records* are thanks to such publicity stunts. While stunts are not used as much today, publicity — essentially free advertising — is still of great value, relatively easy to get, and well worth working on. This chapter will discuss some of the best paths to publicity.

a. Connect with a cause

Many businesses link themselves to local or national causes, invent or sponsor fundraising events, and donate from certain sales promotions, gaining considerable favorable publicity as a result.

b. Be a personality or expert

Bob Stupak, the owner of the Vegas World Hotel and casino in Las Vegas, is the classic model of a business owner creating publicity through his or her own persona. Stupak is often featured in newspapers and magazines, has been profiled on "60 Minutes," and, in total, has reaped millions of dollars worth of free advertising by being a notable, newsworthy, flamboyant personality. He has played high-stakes poker against a supposedly unbeatable poker computer, made the largest known bet on a boxing match at a competing casino — and won, and even run for mayor of Las Vegas. Stupak has put his business on the map with the strength of his own personality.

You don't need to be eligible for "Lifestyles of the Rich and Famous" to take advantage of this type of publicity. There's a dentist who dresses up in a super-hero costume once a week and speaks at schools' health classes as Super Dentist. Every so often, some television newscast picks up on this and gives him some publicity.

If being a "personality" isn't your style but you qualify as an expert on some subject, you can use that to your advantage. Local and national media need a lot of quotable experts. Every year at income tax time a number of accountants and other tax experts get tremendous amounts of free advertising, as they are sought out, interviewed, and quoted by the media. Instead of waiting for this to happen, you can find a way to make it happen.

One florist compiled statistics and lists of interesting and funny reasons why men come in and buy flowers, then let the media know he had compiled all this information. In short order, he was interviewed on a local radio station and quoted in a local magazine. He sent that magazine article around to some national magazines and wound up being quoted in one of the tabloids and in a national women's magazine. He has parleyed this into annual publicity at Valentine's Day time.

To become known as an expert, you can begin by writing some articles and having them published in a trade magazine or newsletter. Fashion magazines are interested in consumer pieces about how you can save money and still be stylish with secondhand fashions, and some consumer magazines and newsletters would certainly consider an article detailing what to look for when purchasing secondhand.

Perhaps you have special knowledge of baseball cards, Raggedy Ann, or Barbie dolls. You can approach your local newspaper with an idea for a story, or even a column if you're really ambitious and confident. Your local paper may welcome free copy from someone who knows what he or she is talking about and who can write. Volunteer to be a speaker for community groups. Every time you stand up in front of a group, people see you and accept you as an expert in the field you are lecturing on. With luck, your efforts will snowball: the more people see you as an expert, the more they want to use you as an authority for events, articles, and television reports, and the more you are used as an authority, the better known as an expert you become.

c. Publicity stunts

Yes, publicity stunts still exist. On Friday the 13th, a record store erected a "superstition obstacle course" in its parking lot, complete with a ladder to walk under, a sidewalk crack to step on, mirrors to break, etc., and then dared all the radio and television personalities to come down and go through the obstacle course. One radio station "bit" and did a live morning drive-time broadcast from the store's site, providing free advertising worth thousands of dollars.

A new country-western nightclub ran a "Dolly Parton look-alike contest" on Parton's birthday, and two out of the four local television stations covered the event. Another nightclub did an "Elvis back from the dead" promotion on Halloween and got television coverage.

d. Holiday tie-ins

There are many opportunities for you to link your business to holidays. People are very conscious of holidays, and the media look for ways to connect their reporting, talk show topics, and features to the holidays. Some secondhand businesses have a built in cache of goodies great for Halloween. Run a "scariest" fashion statement contest with sales staff outfits to sear the eyeballs of any customers. Let the radio and television news departments know what you are doing.

Save all those truly odd Valentine memorabilia through the year and let the news media know about your collection before the 14th.

Set up all your computers to sing Christmas carols. (You will begin to lose staff the second day so limit it to one publicity stunt hour.)

For more discussion of promotion and publicity, see *Getting Publicity*, another title in the Self-Counsel Series.

24
The back office

a. Financial record keeping

Few people enjoy keeping financial records. Most see it as an unpleasant distraction to the main business of running a store.

While it may never become a joy to do, bookkeeping can be made more pleasant (or less unpleasant) by having a good system that you can readily understand.

There are two basic reasons for keeping accurate and up-to-date accounts. Whether you like it or not, the tax department insists that you supply it with certain information at regular intervals — along with a slice of the business profits. Keeping adequate records is not only necessary to comply with the law but to ensure you do not pay one single penny more in taxes than you have to.

A good bookkeeping system should tell you your exact financial position at all times. This will allow you to determine just how much money you are making and where your business is going. If you're heading for trouble, a good system will enable you to spot problems early and take corrective action before it is too late.

Do you need the services of a professional accountant? The answer to this should be no, at least in the beginning stages.

What you do need is a set of records you can understand and maintain yourself. You may need help from your accountant or a bookkeeper in setting it up and you would certainly be wise to have an accountant review your year-end tax return. However, it will save

A good bookkeeping system is vital to the success of your business, letting you know at all times just how much money you are making.

you a lot of money if you can handle your own bookkeeping chores, at least in the beginning stages. Later on, when your business is making a lot of money, you can make your record-keeping system as sophisticated as you want.

Your ease with computers may also dictate your decisions on this aspect of your business. If you are familiar with programs such as Lotus 1-2-3, you may be more comfortable going immediately with such a system. Computerized accounting systems are now within the budget of most business people.

One very important note: if you use a computer, make sure you back up your work on a disk that you keep in another location. If your store is broken into or destroyed by fire, you'll be very happy to have your accounts elsewhere.

b. Setting up a good bookkeeping system

Keeping it inexpensive and simple involves three things:

(a) Do as much of the basic bookkeeping work as possible yourself. It is a waste of money to ask your accountant to total invoices or to make journal entries for you. If your business grows to the point where you can't handle these chores, then consider handing them over to a part-time bookkeeper, or a data entry person if you are using a computerized accounting program.

(b) Hand over the "higher-level" accounting functions and tax matters to your accountant. You should let your accountant show you how to set up and maintain your general ledger and either complete or review your year-end financial statements and income tax return.

(c) Always be up-to-date in your record keeping. Never allow yourself to get so far behind that you are faced with a mountain of backlogged work and the task appears hopeless. Much of the onerous nature of bookkeeping work can be relieved if things are kept current. More important, not being up-to-date can mean that your records are not much use to you. During a critical phase of your business you will have to make decisions based on the latest information. Four- or five-month-old data may not be helpful.

You should retain your bookkeeping records in your possession except when your accountant is actually working on them. This

Accurate records are essential if your business needs to borrow money, either for normal operating requirements or to finance expansion.

Once your business is off and running, you will need an accountant about once a year, chiefly to advise you on your tax return, especially if your business is incorporated.

183

applies especially to your general ledger. This is one of your most valuable business tools; it should be accessible to you at all times. You should not have to call up your accountant to get information that is recorded in your general ledger.

Don't wait for formal financial statements at the end of the month, especially if your business is undergoing changes of any kind (e.g., expansion). Get out your calculator and do a rough financial statement from the general ledger as soon as possible after the end of the month. Ask your accountant to show you how to do this.

c. Income

You need to keep a record of all money received and, if you grant credit, a record of all money owing to you. When something is sold, be it at a flea market or in your own store, make out a sales slip, and be sure to keep a carbon copy for yourself. Alternatively, you may enter the figures neatly in a ruled notebook. In either case, be sure to collect and record separately the sales tax.

Your system should be set up so it gives you good control over cash receipts. Good cash handling and internal control procedures are not only important to you as a business owner or manager, but also to your employees, since a good system shows that employees have handled their responsibilities correctly and honestly.

1. Petty cash

For minor disbursements that have to be handled by cash, a petty cash fund should be established. You should put enough cash into this fund to take care of about one month's transactions. The fund should be the responsibility of one person only. Payments out of it must be supported by a receipt or voucher explaining the purpose of the disbursement.

2. Bank reconciliation

One necessary evil of accurate record keeping is a monthly bank reconciliation. At the end of each month, you will receive a statement from your bank showing each deposit, the amount of each check paid, and other items added to or subtracted from the bank balance. The canceled (paid) checks should accompany this statement. The back of your statement probably contains a reconciliation form that you can follow. If you are still unsure how to manage a bank reconciliation, discuss it with your banker or someone with bookkeeping experience — it's really a lot simpler than it appears at first glance.

3. Invoices and order forms

Use standard blank invoice forms, which can be bought at most large stationery stores, and rubber stamp them with your name, address, and terms of sale.

Buy blank invoice forms in duplicate. Give the original to the customer and keep one copy for your records. Invoices should be numbered consecutively, and your copies should be filed numerically so they are easy to retrieve.

d. Expenses

Keep a detailed record of all your expenses as they occur. Don't rely on your memory to recall amounts you have paid out. Always ask for receipts. At times this is a nuisance, but you must do it if you want the expenditure to count as a business expense. In those few cases where it is not possible to get a receipt (e.g., parking meters and phone booths), jot down the expense in your notebook.

If you attend an out-of-town flea market or fair, take an envelope with you and stuff your receipts for meals, motel bills, gas, etc. into it as you get them. When you get back home, you can sort out the different kinds of expenses and write yourself a business check for those items you have paid for out of cash from your own pocket.

Whenever possible, pay your bills by check so your canceled checks can serve as receipts. Retain all your supplier's invoices. File these away alphabetically in an accordion file or in file folders so you can retrieve them easily if you want to verify expenses, check supplier prices, or terms.

e. Depreciation

If you buy an important piece of equipment, you will need to make a special kind of entry in your records. Real property and equipment constitute fixed assets. It would not be realistic to consider the whole cost of a fixed asset as an expense in any one year. Instead, the cost of the asset is distributed over the period of its useful life. This is known as depreciation of the asset.

In the beginning, when your needs are limited, it is much better to buy all the forms you need ready-made, but once you are using more than 100 or so a month, it's cheaper to get them printed.

Depreciation is an important factor in calculating your year-end profit and income tax. For income tax purposes, various kinds of fixed assets are grouped together in classes and yearly depreciation is allowed at a certain prescribed rate by the tax department. Certain types of production equipment can, for example, be written off in a year or two.

Yearly depreciation rates for the most common types of fixed assets are available from the tax department (the IRS or Revenue Canada) or you can get them from your accountant. The amount you choose to write off in your yearly financial statement may be different from the amount used for income tax purposes. This is a highly complex subject beyond the scope of this book; seek the advice of your accountant.

f. Payroll

If you are employing others or if your business is incorporated, you are responsible for deductions at source from your employees' wages or salaries. You must open an account with the tax department and they will send you a book of tables of the amounts you must deduct for each pay period. To keep track of this, use a separate payroll book with columns for the various types of deductions. These are available in different sizes in most good stationery stores.

g. The general ledger

Each of the columns in your journal will have a separate account or page in your general ledger. Entries in the general ledger are usually made at the end of each month and it is a good idea for you to learn to do this yourself. It is advisable, however, for you to get your accountant to set up the general ledger for you in the beginning and to explain to you how financial statements are taken off. This may involve several fairly lengthy sessions with your accountant, but it is worthwhile. In the long run you will save money. By having a complete understanding of your financial records, you will be able to make your business run more efficiently and make bigger profits.

h. Taxes

One of the main reasons for having a good bookkeeping system is to avoid paying any more taxes than you absolutely have to.

Since the tax laws are not only extremely complex but are constantly being changed, it is essential for any small-business person to seek tax advice from an accountant. However, just as in the area of record keeping, there are quite a number of things you can do yourself to reduce the tax bite.

1. Income

In the area of what to include as income there is not much scope for tax saving. Not declaring income earned from your business is tax fraud, pure and simple. Apart from being illegal, not declaring income can be highly disadvantageous if you are applying for a loan. There may come a time when the continued success or even survival of your business will depend on getting a loan. No respectable lender will give you money on the basis of your word that your financial records have to be seen in the light of the extra income you do not declare on your tax return!

A similar situation would arise if you wanted to sell your business; you couldn't seriously expect a potential buyer to offer a big price for your business on the basis that you cheat on your income tax.

2. Expenses

There is more scope for tax saving in the area of expenses. Keep receipts for all business expenses and personal expenses where any portion of the expense can be charged to your business. Though simple and obvious, this rule is often ignored either because people find it too much trouble to ask for receipts or because they believe certain expenses will be allowed without them.

If it is not too much trouble earning your income in the first place, it certainly isn't too much trouble to ask for a receipt. It's this simple: every time you keep the receipt for $2 spent on postage or parking or whatever, you put another tax-free dollar into your pocket.

There are very few places where you simply cannot get a receipt for expenditures. Where this does happen, as in the case of pay-telephone calls or parking meters, you should keep a diary of these expenses. You would be surprised how some of these minor expenses can add up to quite significant amounts in a year's time.

If you believe you are entitled to claim certain expenses without substantiating receipts, you are completely wrong. Your mistake could turn out to be a costly one. Without receipts, a tax assessor does not have to allow a single cent for your expenses, no matter what they are. In the case of relatively small amounts paid for by cash, you must be particularly careful. While on a sales trip or attending an out-of-town craft market, always ask for and keep all your receipts for meals and lodging. Keep a detailed diary of expenses for parking, postage, pay telephones, and similar small amounts.

(a) Automobile expenses

Both the IRS and Revenue Canada require that all vehicle expenses be recorded and receipts kept. It is not sufficient just to write down expenses incurred when you were actually using the vehicle for business. You must keep the entire year's expenses, including fuel, repairs, insurance, parking, depreciation, interest on the vehicle loan, license, and registration fees.

If you use your vehicle for both business and pleasure, you will need to keep a log showing mileage for both types of use. The total you can claim as business expenses will be based on the percentage of miles you drove for business purposes compared to total miles traveled.

(b) Business expenses in the home

One of the many advantages of operating your secondhand business from your home is the ability to deduct a certain portion of your home expenses, such as heat, rent, taxes, utilities, and mortgage interest. In Canada, mortgage interest payments are not normally deductible for private residences, so anything you can do to make a portion deductible will result in significant tax benefits.

To deduct a portion of your home expenses, you are required to establish that you regularly use a specific part of the home for your secondhand business. Once this is established, you can deduct the portion of items, such as rent, heat, etc., assignable to that portion of the home. But be careful here. To qualify for a tax deduction, a room must be used *solely* for business purposes. You cannot, for example, claim expenses for an "office" that occupies a part of your bedroom.

(c) Maintenance and repairs

Maintenance refers to the routine painting of a building or replacement of parts on machinery and equipment. Repairs means fixing a breakdown or restoring something to normal mechanical condition. The value of a repair can be claimed as a business expense in the year it was incurred.

What happens in the case of very extensive repairs? If you have a flat roof that leaks, you may decide that rather than have it patched up, you will have a pitched roof built over the building. In this case, there will be an addition to the building, even though it was prompted by the need for a repair.

The difference from the tax point of view is that a repair can be claimed as an expense in the current year, while an addition has to be added to the capital cost of the asset and depreciated over a number of years. Also, if the addition is depreciated and the asset is subsequently sold for more than the depreciated value, there is a "recapture" of depreciation and tax has to be paid on the recapture.

Naturally it is to your advantage as a taxpayer to "expense" an item whenever possible. If in doubt about whether an item can be treated this way, check with your accountant.

i. You and your accountant

For tax matters you should seek the services of a professional accountant who can advise you how to minimize tax payable and maximize profit in light of the most recent rules and regulations. These rules and regulations are not only highly complex, they are constantly changing.

As discussed in chapter 11, Professional help, you can minimize the accounting fee by having all your bookkeeping done so that you don't pay a high-priced accountant to do mundane book work you could do yourself. You can also be aware of the various possibilities for tax saving so you will be better prepared to ask your accountant specific questions about what is best in your particular circumstances.

j. Equipping your office

Initially, before you have employees, your "back office" may be right up front by your cash register so you can guard your money. In any case, a bare bones office is all you really need to get started.

1. Basic equipment

- Desk and desk chair
- File cabinet/box
- Small table area for coffee, etc.
- Good light source for the desk
- Computer and printer
- Fax machine
- A clock
- Stationery: pens, paper, envelopes, paper clips, stapler, file folders, a three-ring binder or two, "sticky" notes, message pads, fax paper, invoices, etc.
- Telephone and telephone book
- Daily appointment calendar
- Accounting journals and books
- Calculator
- Sales register

2. Telephone

You can use a basic telephone such as you have at home, but it is recommended that you start with a touch-tone phone with hold, redial, and a speaker phone. If you are trying to track down an item, some of those features can be especially useful.

Since the monthly charge for a business line can be a large expense, check if your phone company has business measured lines. Unlike regular business lines where there is a flat monthly fee regardless of the number of calls you make, the monthly charge for a measured line is lower, but you pay for each outgoing call. Usually a certain number of outgoing calls are free before the per-call charge kicks in, and long-distance calls are not included in your quota.

A business metered line is worth considering if you don't anticipate a huge number of outgoing calls. Incoming calls on a measured line are all free regardless of how many there are. In many cases, the savings in a year can be substantial.

3. Answering machine or service

Who answers the telephone after-hours? People no longer expect to get an endlessly ringing telephone line. They expect some sort of response, even if just an answering machine.

Your message does not have to be long or complicated. A simple greeting with your store's name, operating hours, days of operation, and perhaps general directions if you are hard to locate is all that's needed. You don't even need the capacity to receive messages: you could have an outgoing message only.

Voice mail and call-answer programs offered by most major telephone companies provide extra flexibility and have been steadily dropping in price over the past few years. In the long run they may still be more expensive than a plain answering machine, but are often better suited to business requirements.

4. Computer

A computer with laser printer and the appropriate software has become a standard in any business. Computers are tools that save hours of your time when making up store signs or doing your accounting. Check out night school courses in your area for basic training if you feel at all uncomfortable with computers.

5. Fax machine

Don't go overboard on the bells and whistles for your fax machine. Extras to look for are a paper cutter, memory for when the paper runs out, and a document feeder. You may never use the rest.

You may also want to get a fax installed in your computer. Computer faxes require little training, but you will need a modem as well.

The drawback of computer faxes is that they are less flexible than a manual stand-alone — really they are only one half of a fax machine. While you can receive faxes from any source, you can only fax out documents created on your computer.

25
Risk management

To be successful, you need to understand the basic risks in owning a business and then make your decisions and choices about managing them, minimizing them, or ignoring them. Insurance will protect you from many problems — see chapter 15 for a discussion of important insurance coverage. The following are some of the other major risks your business faces.

a. Accumulation of debt

Manage your debts carefully and do not let them overwhelm your business.

Nothing can sink your business faster than running up a big debt in anticipation of income that never materializes. Those monthly payments to creditors can become a huge burden.

Not only is credit easy to obtain, credit card companies push their cards, and suppliers such as computer and office furniture stores have on-the-spot financing to make purchasing easy. But the interest rates on some of this debt is outrageous. On a $5,000 debt from a department store where the rate can be near 20% per year, you have to pay almost $1,000 each year in interest before you even begin to pay off the principal amount you owe.

Going into debt is one of the most prevalent forms of financial suicide for new companies.

b. Employee theft

It is shocking and, for most business owners, extremely difficult to believe their employees would ever steal from them, yet reliable research indicates that over 80% of all employees steal from their employers!

There are five main categories of employee theft:
(a) Pilferage of merchandise
(b) Pilferage of supplies
(c) Cash theft from the register
(d) Conspiracy with shoplifters
(e) Conspiracy with delivery persons

The first two can seem relatively innocent and unimportant. It's a type of theft we've probably all been guilty of at one time or another ... the executive who takes legal pads, pens, and pencils home for his or her kids or makes photocopies on the office copier for his or her garden club; the retail clerk who drinks a soft drink and eats a package of cookies without paying for them.

"Petty pilferage," left alone, tends to grow, not decline; as employees go undetected in their pilferage, some will be tempted to push the limits even more.

There are three factors driving employee theft: need, the ability to justify the theft, and opportunity. Since just about everybody needs more money and, at certain times, badly needs more money, there's not much you can do to control need. And, because the ability to justify the theft is going on inside the individual's thoughts, there's not a lot you can do to control this either. The owner's prime area of control lies in eliminating opportunity.

There are literally hundreds of ways employees can conceal and cover up thefts. You'll do yourself a big favor by visiting the library and checking out some books on retail theft control and security. Also see *Cut Your Losses*, another book in the Self-Counsel Series. Failure to exercise this kind of control can put you out of business!

c. Employee, partner, or investor disputes

Employee disputes with employers turning into lawsuits seem to be the order of the day. The two most common types of dispute are sexual harassment lawsuits and lawsuits for unjust termination.

There are laws governing hiring, compensation, management, and termination of employees, and you will need to be aware of these rules and regulations if you are going to be an employer.

Obviously, one approach to all this is to minimize the number of people you employ, and many businesses use independent contractors, temporary employees, and part-time employees to simplify their managerial situations. Investigate these options carefully if you want to use them because there are rules and definitions you must be aware of.

Investor disputes need to be avoided at virtually all costs, as they can lead not only to civil lawsuits but to unwanted scrutiny of your business and your relationships with investors by government authorities. Obviously, being fair and forthright with investors in promises and projections will prevent most problems. Communication is the next best problem prevention tool — most people react much worse to being ignored than to losing money or delayed payments.

Partner disputes are best avoided by dissolution, buy-out, and exit terms agreed to far in advance of any problem, just like a pre-nuptial agreement before the wedding.

d. Violation of laws

Ignorance is not bliss, and ignorance of the law is no excuse for violation of the law.

Operating illegally is, quite obviously, a big risk. It's a big shock to many entrepreneurs that they can't just do any darned thing they want to. The "it's my business, I'll do as I please" attitude can get you into a great deal of trouble.

In most states and provinces there are handbooks of business law specific to the area, and they are usually available at public libraries or at a university's law library. Beyond that, if you have any doubts about the legalities of an action you are considering, you should consult with your lawyer or the appropriate government agency.

The unpleasant truth is that we do live in an increasingly complex society, and the days of just hanging up your shingle, putting some stock on the shelves, and conducting business are long since gone.

e. Heightened competition

Probably the most common universal risk of business is the appearance of some new, sharp, innovative, aggressive, better-financed competitor. The first rule of survival is to pick your battle, to avoid the likelihood of having to bare knuckles and duke it out with somebody a lot bigger and tougher and possibly better than you are. Another answer is to devise a combination of goods, services, and qualities that is truly unique and difficult to battle head-on. Offer something your competitor cannot do better.

If you are a gregarious and knowledgeable antique dealer, play to those strengths. Build unshakeable customer loyalty through superior service and personal attention so you protect your customer base no matter what happens around you.

f. Sudden changes in the economy

If you are prepared for the possibility of economic downdrafts, they can be a terrific opportunity for any secondhand business. First, there is a plethora of product as businesses and their employees tighten up. During times like these, cash is king. If you have the foresight to keep a bit of liquid reserves, you can do very well on the buying end.

You can do well on the selling end, too, if you sharpen your buying skills. You will have more customers, not fewer, as the economy skids. People still have to dress for the office, still need computers, still must have all the accoutrements of life, just at a cheaper-than-new price.

Secondhand stores and bankruptcy lawyers do better in down times. The exception is high-priced antique stores. For antiques, the buying may get better as your high-end customers are likely to be unaffected; middle class dabblers, however, tend to slow down on collecting. Still, if you double your marketing, especially using your prospect lists, even antique stores can do well buying at distress prices and selling to high-end clients.

g. Bad debt and collection problems

Letting the money owed to your business build up and sneak out of control is a major risk — in fact, it destroys an enormous number of businesses. Beyond allowing your customer to buy now and pay later — a policy that has sunk more than one business — there are hidden forms of credit such as checks and credit cards.

You are not a bank and cannot permit others to use you as a bank. This has nothing whatsoever to do with trusting or not trusting a customer, liking or not liking a customer, or being nice or nasty. It simply has everything to do with the core nature of your business and your defined relationships with your customers.

You control this risk by being very clear, firm, and tough about extending credit policies from the very beginning. It's easier to be tough from the outset than to get tough later. And, if the only way you can get a customer is by extending loose, liberal credit, you're better off letting that customer move on down the road — where he or she will ultimately be a collection problem for one of your competitors.

If you accept all major credit cards, it's easy and convenient for customers to pay you. Just be sure to follow the rules exactly. Without an imprint of the card and a verified signature, you might be giving away your goods. Without both, the customer can claim they did not receive the goods ordered and the credit card company will side with the customer every time. This means you will have to chase the person to collect. For small items this may not be worth your time. (Chapter 18 discusses forms of payment in further detail.)

Checks are a little more obvious. All the identification in the world does not make a check valid. It can still bounce, leaving you with the rotten option of chasing someone for money. Get to know your clients and insist on cash if you are at all unsure.

Depending on your volume of check business, you might find it wise to get check insurance. It is relatively cheap, between ½% and 1½% of the value of the checks, for the piece of mind that it brings.

Appendix 1

RESOURCES

There is an enormous range of reference books and publications available, covering every imaginable type of product. Your local library will be an invaluable source of information, but the following lists will give you a brief overview of what to expect. It's also important to remember that many secondhand dealers come to rely as much on their accumulated knowledge as on books.

a. Reference books

The Barbie Doll Years by Patrick C. Olds (ISBN: 0-89145-759-3).

Book Collecting: A Comprehensive Guide by Allen Ahearn (ISBN: 0-39913-456-5).

Collector's Guide to Art Deco, Identification and Values by Mary Frank Gaston (ISBN: 0-89145-769-0).

Flea Market Trader by Sharon and Bob Huxford (ISBN: 0-89145-779-8).

Kovels' Guides; published annually by Crown Trade Paperbacks (Random House). These pricing guides cover everything from silver and silver marks to bottles and Royal Doulton.

The Official Beckett Price Guide to Baseball Cards by Dr. James Beckett (ISBN: 0-676-60050-6).

Official Price Guide to Antiques and Collectibles published by the House of Collectibles, NY.

Silver Marks of the World by Jan Divis (ISBN: 0-600-38156-0).

Unit's Canadian Price Guide Antiques 15 Collectibles published annually by Fitzhenry and Whiteside.

Warman's Antiques and Collectibles Price Guide published by Wallace Homestead Book Company.

b. Newsletters

Kovels on Antiques and Collectibles
PO Box 420349
Palm Coast, FL 32142-9655

A monthly guide to prices, trends, auction results, and other issues.

The Resale Connection
Box 562
Palm Harbor, FL 34682
Tel: 813-786-7047
US$28 for 12 issues.

Appendix 2

FRANCHISE OPPORTUNITIES

Cash Converters Canada Inc.
1131A Leslie Street, Penthouse Suite
Toronto, ON M3C 3L8
Tel: 416-449-9454
Fax: 416-449-9412

Cash Converters USA
1350 Zurich Towers
1450 East American Lane
Schaumburg, IL 60173
Tel: 847-330-1122
Fax: 847-330-1660

Grow Biz International
4200 Dahlberg Drive
Minneapolis, MN 55422-4837
Tel: 612-520-8500
Fax: 612-520-8410
Toll-free: 1-800-433-2540

Grow Biz International has five different franchises:
  (a) Play it Again Sports
  (b) Disk Around
  (c) Music Around
  (d) Once Upon a Child
  (e) Computer Renaissance

Sports Traders
Traders International Management Inc.
508 Discovery Street
Victoria, BC V8T 1G8
Tel: 250-383-6443
Fax: 250-383-8481
Toll-free: 1-800-792-3111

The Used Computer Store
Corporate Office
99 Bronte Road, Suite 111
Oakville, ON L6L 3B7
Tel: 905-825-5000
Fax: 905-847-8844
Toll-free: 1-888-665-0055

OTHER BUSINESS TITLES FROM SELF-COUNSEL PRESS

GETTING PUBLICITY

The very best book for your small business
Tana Fletcher and Julia Rockler
$14.95

If you dream of getting publicity for your small business, your organization, or yourself, you need this book. Step-by-step instructions illustrate just what it takes to attract media attention to any enterprise. The authors, both award-winning journalists, show how to make the most of every opportunity for free coverage in the print and broadcast media, and how to handle the resulting interviews with ease. This new and expanded edition included advice on radio apprearances and a new section answers frequently asked questions.

Regardless of your budget or your background, with this book you can learn how to sparkle in the media spotlight. Aimed specifically at individuals and organizations whose ambitions are bigger than their bankrolls, *Getting Publicity* emphasizes low cost, do-it-yourself promotional strategies, and is filled with inexpensive and practical tips for capitalizing on the power of publicity.

READY-TO-USE BUSINESS FORMS

Give your business a professional look
Save time and money ... we've designed the forms for you
Impress your customers with your new image
$13.95

Running an efficient small business can be simplified if effective systems are in place and the paperwork is up-to-date. Standardized business forms establish and maintain these important systems.

The sample forms in this handy book can be torn out to be quickprinted or photocopied as needed. It includes dozens of basic forms that every small business requires for its day-to-day operations, plus special poster forms and artwork for announcements and publicity purposes. Included inside are forms for:

- Memos
- Meeting Agendas
- Long Distance Telephone Logs
- Employee Performance Reviews
- Standard Application for Employment
- Vacation Schedule
- Invoice and Statement sales forms
- Purchase Orders and Purchase Order Records
- Stock Record and Inventory form
- 52-Week chart and 31-Day chart
- ... plus many, many, more

PREPARING A SUCCESSFUL BUSINESS PLAN

A practical guide for small business
Rodger Touchie, B.Comm., M.B.A.
$14.95

At some time, every business needs a formal business plan. Whether considering a new business venture, or rethinking an existing one, an effective plan is essential to success. From start to finish, this working guide outlines how to prepare a plan that will win potential investors and help acheive business goals.

Recognizing that a business plan constitutes much more than the written document, this book will enable you to lay the foundation for a dynamic process of planning, reviewing, and updating your business agenda.

Using worksheets and a sample plan, readers learn how to create an effective business plan, establish planning and maintenance methods, and update their strategy in response to actual business conditions.

Contents include:

- The basic elements of business planning
- Other types of plans: marketing and financial
- Creating a planning team
- Writing concluding remarks and statements
- Preparing an executive summary
- Presenting an impressive document
- Common misconceptions in business planning
- Using a business plan as a tangible asset
- Developing an ongoing role for future planning

ORDER FORM

All prices are subject to change without notice. Books are available in book, department, and stationery stores. If you cannot buy the book through a store, please use this order form. (Please print)

Name _____

Address _____

_____

Charge to: ❑ Visa   ❑ MasterCard

Account Number _____

Validation Date _____

Expiry Date _____

Signature _____

❑ Check here for a free catalog.

YES, please send me:

_____ *Preparing A Successful Business Plan*
_____ *Ready-To-Use Business Forms*
_____ *Getting Publicity*

IN THE U.S.A.
Please send your order to:
Self-Counsel Press Inc.
1704 N. State Street
Bellingham, WA 98225

IN CANADA
Please send your order to the nearest location:
Self-Counsel Press
1481 Charlotte Road
North Vancouver, BC V7J 1H1

4 Bram Court
Brampton, ON L6W 3R6

Please add $3.00 for postage & handling.
Canadian residents, please add 7% GST to your order.
Washington residents, please add 7.8% sales tax.

Visit our Web site at: *www.self-counsel.com*